EXPLORING NEW MEXICO WINE COUNTRY

New Mexico: The Cradle of North American Wine

The water wheel at historic Salman Ranch, north of Las Vegas, ground flour for the the U.S. Calvary at old Ft. Union. The restored mill is one of many attractions on the Northern Winery Tour.

EXPLORING NEW MEXICO WINE COUNTRY

New Mexico: The Cradle of North American Wine

by Babs Suzanne Harrison
& Staefan Eduard Rada

Including Special Sections on
The Microbreweries of New Mexico
and
New Mexico Wine Festivals

Cover & Illustrations by
Bruce F. Finney

Coyote Press
Los Cerrillos, New Mexico

Published by: Coyote Press
              Box 267
              Los Cerrillos, New Mexico   87010

Publisher's Cataloging-in-publication Data:

Harrison, Babs Suzanne
    Exploring New Mexico Wine Country: New Mexico, the cradle of North Ameri-
can Wine/ Babs Suzanne Harrison & Staefan Eduard Rada; cover & illustrations by
Bruce F. Finney. Los Cerrillos, N.M. : Coyote Press, 1994.
    p. : ill., maps

    "Including special sections on the microbreweries of New Mexico and New
Mexico wine festivals."
    Includes index.

1.   Wineries—New Mexico—Guidebooks.   2.   Wine and wine
making—New   Mexico—History. 3. Breweries—New Mexico—Guidebooks.
4. Festivals—   New Mexico—Guidebooks. 5. New Mexico—Description
and travel—Guide   books.   I. Rada, Staefan Eduard. II. Finney,
Bruce F.   III. Title.

917.8956 1994   Library of Congress Catalog Card Number: 94-68640
ISBN 1-886023-09-3 $12.95 Softcover

Illustrations and cover by Bruce F. Finney

Interior design by Anna Martinez

Printed in the United States of America

For information on ordering see back of book.

Other works by these authors:

THE LION IN THE MOON: *TWO AGAINST THE SAHARA*

A NOTE OF APPRECIATION

Special thanks to Richard and Shirley Jones, Henry Street, Dotty Griffith, Marc Simmons, and Jerry Dorbin for their assistance and instructive comments in the preparation of this manuscript.

This book would have been impossible without the enthusiastic participation of the wine makers and brewmasters of New Mexico. Our thanks to all.

Finally, a special citation to Bruce Finney's artistic talent. His illustrations are worth several thousand of our words.

--BSH & SER

TABLE OF CONTENTS

MAPS

1

NUEVO MEXICO: EL NACIMIENTO DEL VINO NORTEAMERICANO

(New Mexico: The Cradle of North American Wine)

The Roots of Wine

Slightly more than a hundred years ago, the southern Rio Grande valley of New Mexico was so heavily planted in vineyards there were few other crops in sight.

Grapes hung from vines in such profusion, according to an article in an El Paso newspaper that, even after the coyotes had crept from the surrounding hills in the dead of night to gorge themselves, New Mexico could proudly proclaim itself the oldest and, for a few short years, the most prolific wine producing region in the United States.

The story of New Mexico wine begins with the first Spanish incursions into the Southwest in the 16th century (eighty years before the Pilgrims landed at Plymouth Rock), and has continued unabated, with the exception of the Prohibition era, for over 360 years, through four distinct historic periods: Spanish Colonial (1598-1820), Mexican (1821-1848), Territorial (1849-1911), and Statehood (from 1912).

It is little known today, but New Mexico wine production preceded that of California by at least one hundred years. The first California mission at San Diego was established by Father Junípero Serra in 1769; the mission at Monterey in 1770. With these missions began the California wine industry now personified by the Napa and Sonoma Valleys.

As the Monterey mission was opening its doors in California, across the continent in Massachusetts British troops were firing into a Boston mob killing five. It would be remembered as the Boston Massacre.

The First Continental Congress in 1774, was calling for civil disobedience to protest British oppression. A year later, the Second Continental Congress named George Washington Commander-in-Chief of the Continental Army. The following year witnessed the signing of the Declaration of Independence.

Meanwhile, back in New Mexico, Spanish Franciscan priests, with the help of local Pueblo Indians, had been harvesting Mission grapes and pressing wine for nearly 140 years at most of the twenty-six missions scattered up and down the Rio Grande (the Great River).

On Horses They Came

Cortez and his men invaded Mexico in 1518 on sixteen horses. Coronado rode into New Mexico twenty years later with over 1,000 horses bred from the finest Spanish stock.

The ancestors of these horses, called Barbs (in reference to the Barbary Coast of Africa), were bred by the Moors on the windswept wastelands of North Africa.

While the English and Dutch directed their colonization efforts with a frontal assault on the east coast of the United States, and the French were probing the Mississippi River, the Spanish entered the American Southwest through the back door, via Mexico.

In 1518, Hernán Cortez sailed from Cuba to carry out the conquest of Mexico. Within two years he had subdued the Aztec empire and established Mexico City as the heart of New Spain (the Spanish name for Mexico). New Spain became the springboard for exploration into New Mexico, as the Spanish labeled the land north of present day Juarez/El Paso.

Twenty years later, Francisco Vásquez de Coronado, accompanied by 292 men, 3 women, 1,300 Indian allies, 1,000 horses, 600 pack animals and a handful of Franciscan priests, set off for what is now Arizona.

Coronado's party wintered near the present-day town of Bernalillo, just north of Albuquerque and close to the great 1,200-room pueblo of Kuaua. Eventually, the explorer strayed as far east as Kansas, and west to the Grand Canyon, before turning back to Mexico City after years of wandering in "the great wilderness," as he described it. A dejected Coronado reported that for all his trouble, he saw "nothing of value."

When the Moors invaded Spain, their horses came along. The Spanish, in turn, exported the Barbs to Mexico and Florida.

Those horses arriving in New Mexico and Texas from Mexico were known as Mustangs. Those flowing into Florida, the Carolinas and Virginia were called Chickasaw. The modern Western descendants of the original North African Barbs and the first Spanish Mustangs is the Quarter Horse.

What Coronado and later Spanish explorers did accomplish, as they followed the Indian trails along the Rio Grande (flowing out of the Colorado Rockies south through the heart of New Mexico to El Paso, and then southeast to form the border between Texas and Mexico, and into the Gulf of Mexico) was to establish *El Camino Real*—The Royal Road or King's Highway.

The name *Camino Real* was assigned by the Spanish to any major road whether in Spain or the New World. Hence, there are several *El Camino Reals* in North America, including the one that connected the missions of California.

By 1598, with Don Juan de Oñate's expedition into New Mexico—Oñate was given official permission by Philip II, King of Spain, to conquer New Mexico—the King's Highway was fully delineated. It ran 1,800

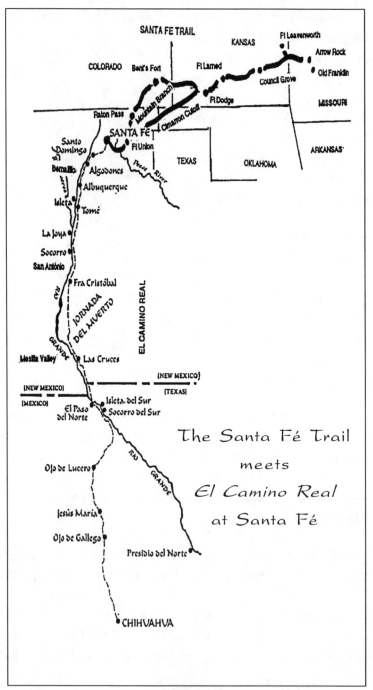

The Santa Fé Trail
meets
El Camino Real
at Santa Fé

miles from Mexico City up through Chihuahua City, across the great desert to El Paso, north through Las Cruces, Socorro, and Albuquerque into Santa Fé, which by 1610 had been officially established as the capital of New Mexico.

With the opening of the 800-mile Santa Fé Trail in 1821, goods from Missouri wholesale houses could move westward, connect with *El Camino Real* at Santa Fé, and flow south into Mexico.

Another stream of goods, including gold dust and nuggets from the Ortiz Mountains south of Santa Fé and silver pesos from Chihuahua, (and sometimes table grapes and wine from the Rio Grande Valley) flowed north to Santa Fé then eastward along the Trail into Missouri.

New Mexico wine, however, was more likely to be drunk enroute under the label of Pass Whiskey (whiskey sold to those 'passing' through). At two dollars a gallon, it was an adulterated variation of grape brandy. Lacking the kick of the real McCoy, Pass Whiskey was often enhanced by early traders in exotic ways. One recipe included tobacco, red hot chile peppers and black gunpowder.

This concoction was consumed the length of the Santa Fé Trail and was a favorite of Indians who sometimes complained, when they got hold of Kentucky whiskey, that the real stuff was too weak.

Eventually, New Mexico table grapes and wine were shipped as far as New York City, particularly after the arrival of the Santa Fe Railroad in 1880. The railroad, as an efficient conveyor of goods, effectively displaced the arduous overland routes. *El Camino Real,* as well as the Santa Fé

Recipe For Pass Whiskey

Ingredients:
 Tobacco
 Grape brandy
 Water
 Chile peppers
 Black gunpowder

Boil some tobacco in a small can of water. Do the same with hot, red chile peppers. Strain both. Add the tobacco and chile juices in equal amounts to a bottle of grape brandy, wine or corn whiskey (if you've got

Trail, receded into the dustbin of history leaving only faint traces of wagon ruts on the New Mexican landscape.

In its 300 years of usage, *El Camino Real*, aside from bearing the distinction, at one point in history, of being the single longest road in North America, was also one of the most grueling. Hundreds lost their lives to thirst and flash floods. The blazing sun shone with white hot intensity for weeks on end only to be interrupted by torrential downpours that filled arroyos (dry gullies) with swirling, muddy waters, sweeping men and livestock to their deaths.

it). Add a pinch of black gunpowder. (Stay away from an open fire in case you get the jitters.) Shake the bottle real good. Pass it around.

A ninety-mile stretch between what is now Las Cruces and Socorro became known as *Jornada del Muerto* (Journey of the Dead) due to countless lives lost to thirst in the barren desert. The land was devoid of water, shelter or fuel; forced night marches were often necessary to ensure survival.

Rustic wood crosses, supported by piles of stones, "were thickly scattered over the country from one end of it to the other" marking the site of a traveler's death. So wrote Lt. James Abert of the Army Topographical Engineers in 1846.

With *El Camino Real* came the Franciscan priests bringing Catholicism and salvation to the indigenous peoples of New Spain and New Mexico. Priests were assigned to each Pueblo and soon put the Indians to work building missions and often wineries for the production of sacramental wine using the latest technology: hammers, wedges, chisels and saws.

From 1609 onward, official caravans came north from Mexico City every three or four years to resupply the growing number of missions. A typical caravan might consist of thirty or forty two-and four-wheel wagons drawn by teams of six-to-twenty oxen plodding along at six-to-eight miles per day. Lighter loads were carried by trains of 200 or more mules, each capable of carrying up to 400 pounds and covering 12-15 miles a day.

Buried in the back of those creaking, wood wagons mixed with the massive cargos of tools, blankets, Bibles, church vestments and even, on occasion, 200-pound bronze bells, were bundles of sticks in wet dirt, wrapped in cloth and carefully husbanded by the Franciscans. These were the grapevine cuttings from Spain, via Mexico City, to establish the first vineyards in the United States.

From these vineyards would be made the sacramental wine required for each mission, and if there were an excess of grapes, a small profit might be made as well. If successful, no longer would it be necessary to import sacramental wine from Spain and Mexico City, which in any case traveled poorly, arriving at the missions in crude tin flasks often reduced to vinegar after years enroute.

It is said the first vineyard was established in 1630, at San Antonio de Padua, south of present day Albuquerque, near Socorro, at the site of the Senecu Indian Pueblo. These first vines are thought to be of the species *Vitus Vinifera* from a seedling of the Monica, a variety common in Spain and similar to the South American grape called *Criolla di vino*, which was also carried to the southern hemisphere by Spanish missionaries.

The Mission grape, as it is more commonly known, is blue in color with a high sugar content and can grow to considerable size. For wine purposes, it lacks acidity and color but is acceptable as a dessert wine. Its vigor and hardiness to disease and adverse climate made it ideal for the New Mexico experiment. Original rootstock can still

---

Weaving Through New Mexico History

Coronado brought 5,000 *churro* sheep with him to New Mexico in 1540. Oñate imported another 3,000 when he settled the land in 1598. The Spanish also brought indigo dyes and European designs and techniques that were assimilated by the Pueblo Indians.

By 1650, the Navajo had adopted the *churro* wool, dyes and designs of the

be found in many small family vineyards up and down the Rio Grande.

Within three years the vineyards at Mission San Antonio, and others along the river, were producing a crop of small, dark grapes on short, sturdy vines. The vines were kept short, near the ground, and covered with dirt and straw in the winter to protect against frost and freezing.

Harvesting the crop meant hours of stoop labor for which the Franciscans employed the nearby Pueblo Indians. Winemaking was crude. Hollowed-out rocks were sometimes used for crushing and dried ox hides were hung from poles for fermentation.

The wine maker would take a raw ox hide and form it into a sack by fastening the outer edges of the hide to a wood form and allow it to dry in the sun until it was like iron. Leather crushing pans were made by drawing a piece of green hide over a square box.

Spanish to create their own weaving traditions that were to shape the cultural development of the Navajo for the next 350 years.

In the 1850s, the introduction of aniline and synthetic dyes and purebred Merino sheep, whose greasy fleece was difficult to hand spin and dye, radically altered the weavings of the Pueblo and Navajo.

In 1880, when the railroad introduced cheaper textiles from the east coast, New Mexico's weaving tradition began to fade. Today, it is carried on mostly by small groups of Navajo and a few Spanish families.

When the hide had dried, it was perforated with holes to allow the juice from the mashed grapes to drain into the hide sack hanging below.

A wood brace was constructed and the dried hide was suspended inside the brace with the crushing pan over the mouth. Grapes were loaded into the pan and the crusher, often a Pueblo Indian, would climb atop the pan and, holding onto a rope suspended from the ceiling for support, would walk about crushing the grapes.

The juice was poured into barrels or clay jugs and allowed to remain about ten days for 'hot' fermentation. Then the juice was drawn off and placed in other barrels for sixty days. It was drained again in a 'cool state.' Thirty days after the second draining the wine was ready for consumption.

The Spanish pronounced *el vino* "excellent," and the San Antonio vineyards continued to produce for another forty years until the 1670s when the mission was attacked by Apache Indians killing the priest and many local Indians.

In 1680, a general uprising of the Pueblo Indians forced the Spanish invaders and Franciscans south out of New Mexico for twelve years, destroying the fledgling wine industry in the process. When the Spanish reconquered the lands in 1693, the vines returned and the Mission grape flourished again.

The beginning of commercial production of wine began with the return of settlers to the Rio Grande Valley after 1693, but against the wishes of the Spanish King, who upon learning of the quality of New Mexican wine, forbade commercial plantings out of fear of competition with Spanish wines.

Contrary to royal decree, the serious cultivation of grapes spread north out of El Paso toward Las Cruces, westward into the Mesilla Valley, and then upriver along the Rio Grande into Socorro, Isleta, Albuquerque and eventually as far north as Santa Fé.

For the next hundred years, until the end of the Spanish colonial period in 1820, little was reported on vineyards except for the diaries of Franciscan priests and occasional military documents that described in sparse terms the presence of vineyards and ample wine.

Deflating Pilgrims' Pride

The first Thanksgiving was held by the Pilgrims in Massachusetts in the Fall of 1621. Or so you've thought. More precisely, the first Thanksgiving was held twenty-three years earlier on the banks of the Rio Grande in what is now Texas, in April of 1598.

Juan de Oñate's party, on their mission to explore and claim

One report in 1766, by a Spanish engineer, noted: "the people make pretty good wine and even better brandy." He was concerned that the inhabitants were not raising enough corn because "they use all the land for vineyards."

Zebulon Montgomery Pike recorded in his 1807 journal seeing "numerous vineyards from which were produced the finest wine ever drank in the country and was the only wine used on the table of the commanding general." He listed the price of a barrel of wine at $15.00.

Pedro Bautista Pino, a wealthy Santa Fé resident, wrote in 1812, "In no other country in America can wine be found with the taste and bouquet of the wine of New Mexico." One trader, who traveled the Santa Fé Trail in the 1820s, noted that New Mexican wine "was a good article, superior to many of the wines that are imported from Europe."

New Mexico for Spain, verging on exhaustion and death, struggled across the Rio Grande to be met by local Manso Indians, who offered duck, fish from the river, and wild grains.

The Spaniards, spared almost certain starvation, hosted their deliverers at a Thanksgiving dinner and Mass. Later that afternoon, Oñate claimed all the lands drained by the Rio Grande for the King of Spain.

Lt. Abert reported in 1846, on reaching the Pueblo of Isleta, (south of Albuquerque) seeing "extensive vineyards with long sheds, under which were ranged huge bloated bags of oxhide, where several Indians were at work distilling the liquors from the vats."

Among the early immigrants was Joseph Tondre, who came to New Mexico from Alsace-Lorraine in 1864. He was instructed by Santa Fé's Archbishop Lamy, himself a Frenchman, (and subject of Willa Cather's *Death Comes for the Archbishop*) to settle at the Pueblo of Isleta. By 1870, Tondre had bought 50 acres of rich river land and had planted 30,000 grapevines.

One Elias Brevoort wrote in 1874, "Those experienced in the cultivation of the wine present that all the conditions of the soil, humidity and temperature, are united in these regions to produce the grape in the greatest perfection. . . . The probability is that as a grape-growing and wine producing section it will be second only to California."

It was recorded in 1789 that 139 shippers sent 600 barrels of wine, brandy and vinegar down *El Camino Real* to Mexico. One thousand, six hundred gallons of wine were produced in 1812, with Rio Grande Valley wineries producing 10,000 gallons annually by 1868. With the coming of Italian Jesuits in the 1860s, however, wine production matured.

When the Atchison, Topeka and Santa Fe Railroad steamed into Albuquerque in 1880, wine production was recorded at 908,000 gallons, outranking New York in both acreage and production. In the next twenty years most every small farm in the valley was in the grape business.

By this time, in addition to the Mission grape, other varieties were being harvested as well, including the Muscatel and certainly the native American grape, the Concord (or something similar), of the genus *Vitis labrusca.*

New Mexico rose to fifth place among the nation's top wine producing regions attracting investors from across the country. It was reported in 1886, that one acre of land with 1,000 vines was worth $1,000. It was also reported in the same year that 10,000 baskets of table grapes were shipped by train to eastern markets.

The Decline of New Mexico Wine

A good thing was not to last. Between 1890-1920, a variety of events

Adobe

as

Architecture

The conquering Spanish melded the sand and clay mud of the Pueblo Indians with the brick form of Europe to produce the adobe brick. These bricks, measuring 10 X 18 X 5 inches and weighing fifty pounds each, made possible the mission church, a building that dwarfed anything the Pueblo Indians had built to date.

including over-production, the high cost of access to markets, drought, flooding and finally prohibition crippled the industry.

A major problem was the limited ability to store and transport wine to distant markets. There was no wood in the whole region from which casks could be manufactured. Nor was there a factory to make bottles. Containers were imported from the east and used over and over, or Mexican-style clay water jugs were used with the throat sealed after filling.

Wine, as a rule, does not travel well, often arriving as vinegar (which is why sulfites are added to stabilize modern wines). Without refrigeration, neither do grapes fare well, although they were usually shipped in the cooler fall after the harvest.

The New Mexico market was small by eastern standards and quickly saturated. Local producers were forced to export. But where? California produced all the wine it needed. Arizona, Utah, Colorado and Texas were sparsely settled. East coast markets were too distant and costly. The rapid growth of the wine industry quickly consumed available labor creating a shortage. In any event, it was back-breaking work. Increasingly, grapes rotted on the vine.

Then in the 1890s, a series of droughts caused the water table to drop. Increased irrigation in Colorado and northern New Mexico drained water from the Rio Grande causing a lowering of the river downstream.

Faced with a lack of traditional building materials, the Franciscan priests united the native materials of rock, mud and logs; the Pueblo flat-roofed style; and the thick, sometimes thirty foot-high walls; and the cruciform floorplan of the Spanish cathedral to create a new Southwestern architectural form.

The rounded adobe shapes of the fortress-like mission church have captured the imagination of generations of visitors and given the Southwest a unique spiritual icon that not only represents New Mexico's 400-year multi-cultural past but speaks powerfully to the future.

Drought was followed by massive flooding in 1897, when the Rio Grande rampaged over its banks to wash away thousands of acres of prime vineyards.

At the turn of the century, farmers began to plow under their vineyards for more profitable crops like cotton, alfalfa and chile peppers. Prohibition in 1920 was the final blow.

While mission wineries survived, as well as many family winemaking operations, the commercial ventures dried up. Thousands of vine stock were uprooted from the earth and burned as firewood. The wine industry in New Mexico was to lay fallow for over forty-five years before the renaissance began.

The Renaissance Of New Mexico Wine

The flame of New Mexican wine was not quite extinguished by prohibition, although decades of neglect would take time to overcome. The rising reputation of California wines along with the general social trend toward lighter beverages provided the sparks needed to rekindle interest in New Mexican vineyards. It made sense, after all, to return to the cradle of American wine.

All the necessary ingredients for successful wine production were present: sunny days with favorable night-day contrasts in temperature; sandy-loam soil; an arid, high desert climate; river irrigation and a general absence of harmful bugs and diseases.

The New Mexico sun is very intense due to a cloudless and arid high mountain desert climate. Elevations range from 3,500 feet in the southern wine region around Las Cruces, which provides for a long growing season of 219 frost-free days, to 6,500 feet in the northern region surrounding Santa Fé, with a shorter growing season. Virgin soils vary from deep clay loams in the south, with a thirty percent sand content, ideal for drainage, to shallow sandy loams over a rocky volcanic base in the north.

Rainfall statewide averages only nine inches annually but an extensive irrigation network fed by the Rio Grande and man-made lakes provides viticulturists with a reliable source of water. The high altitude guarantees nighttime temperatures will drop 30-35 degrees below those of the daytime enabling vinifera and hybrid grapes in New Mexico to maintain a high acid to high sugar balance.

In the mid-to-late '60s grapes began to make their comeback in small plots planted by amateur winemakers. Basement operations led to a growing recognition by a discerning segment of the public that indeed, the return of New Mexico wine was not only possible, but probable.

In the '70s, the first tentative steps toward commercial wine production had begun with the importation of cuttings from California by farmers looking for alternatives to water intensive crops such as cotton and sorghum.

European vintners, frustrated by small plots, high land prices, and government regulations that limited production in their home countries, took notice of the potential of New Mexico where suitable land could be obtained for $1,000 an acre compared to nearly $15,000 in California.

Canadian, French, German and Swiss consortia began buying thousand-acre tracts in the lower Rio Grande Valley for test vineyards. Upriver, around Belen, Albuquerque, Bernalillo and even further north to Santa Fé, Los Alamos and Dixon, American growers were purchasing and planting smaller tracts with hardy French hybrids.

By the late '70s, there were at least five boutique wineries in the state, although the vineyards were small with less than 100 acres under cultivation. By the early '80s, acreage had increased to 500; wineries to ten.

At this point, acreage and volume began to increase dramatically. There were twelve wineries by 1984, with 4,000 acres under cultivation, comparable to state production one hundred years earlier, in the 1880s. In 1987, over 700,000 gallons of wine were produced.

By latest count, there are eighteen active wineries in New Mexico, with over 5,000 acres of vinestock, producing well over a million gallons of wine annually.

A Primer On Grapes

It is important to remember that there are grapes, and then there are grapes. Not all wine comes from grapes; not all grapes make wine. There are eating grapes and juice grapes, perhaps as many as 5,000 varieties. And there are wine grapes, a much smaller, more select fraternity of about fifty major varieties.

All grapes fall into the biological genus *Vitis*. Only two of the many Vitis species are used for wine, *Vitis Vinifera* and *Vitis Labrusca*. Viniferas are the great European wine grapes, such as the French Cabernets and Chardonnays, and the German Rieslings. Most of the world's wines—and all the great wines—are produced from pure vinifera stock.

The second category, *Vitis Labrusca*, is the native American grape, such as the Concord, which is often used for juice and jelly. Some American wineries have produced a hybrid of French *Vinifera* and American *Labrusca*, combining the flavor of the former with the hardiness of the latter. These French hybrids have been introduced into regions of the United States where harsh winters would kill off the pure stock varieties.

Of these fifty varieties of wine grapes, less than twenty are relied on for most wines. And of the twenty, the most popular white grape is the Chardonnay and the most popular red is the Cabernet Sauvignon, although another red, the Pinot Noir, is the foundation for all great red Burgundies.

Major Red Wine Vinifera Grapes

CABERNET FRANC	Often blended with Cabernet Sauvignon in parts of France and northern Italy.
CABERNET SAUVIGNON	Popular French and California variety
CARIGNAN	The most common grape of France.
GAMAY	The backbone of French Beaujolais. Not to be confused with California's Gamay

	Beaujolais, which is not a Gamay, but a knock-off of Pinot Noir.
GRENACHE	A common, sweet, French grape found in Provence.
MERLOT	Usually blended with Cabernet Sauvignon in both France and California but may stand alone.
NEBBIOLO	The backbone grape of northern Italy. Rarely planted outside of Italy.
PINOT NOIR	Source of all great red burgundies. Important for Champagne. Primarily French but Oregon now recognized as a strong producer.
SYRAH	The principal red grape of France's Rhine Valley. Produces a dark, strong wine.
SANGIOVESE	A red grape of Italian origin.
ZINFANDEL	Principally a California variety. Thought to originate in southern Italy.

Major White Wine Vinifera Grapes

ALIGOT	Common white grape of the Burgundy region of France.
CHARDONNAY	Basic to most great white burgundies and champagne. The most successful California wine grape.
CHENIN BLANC	A French grape from the Loire Valley.
GEWÜRZTRAMINER	A German 'spicy' grape often served as an aperitif. Found in the cooler climates of California, Oregon and Washington.
MUSCAT CANELLI	A wine grape of exceptional sweetness and aroma. Produced in many parts of the world, including California, and is sometimes served as a dessert wine. Introduced into New Mexico in the 1880s.

PINOT BLANC	While grown in Burgundy and California, the grape is more closely associated with *Pinot Bianco* wine of northern Italy.
RIESLING	Basis for the finest white wines of Germany. Does well in the coolest regions of California.
SAUVIGNON BLANC	Grown widely around the world, including California, and is the basis for many blended wines. Often is sold under the name *Fumé Blanc* in California.
SÉMILLON	Often mixed with Sauvignon Blanc to form the basis for the sweet *Sauternes* of France. An expensive and carefully made wine, it stands alone for its uniqueness. (Not to be confused with the sweet wine made in California of the same name aimed at the 'low end' of the wine market.)

Wine may be made from a single variety such as Cabernet Sauvignon or Chardonnay, which is common in the great wine regions of Europe and in regions of California, or the juice from several varieties may be blended together to form a varietal wine, such as when Merlot is blended with Cabernet Sauvignon, or when two whites are blended, such as Sémillon and Sauvignon Blanc.

Lastly, consider that sometimes the color of the grape is misleading. Red grapes often form the basis for a white wine. For instance, the red Pinot Noir is the heavy weight for all good Burgundies. Remove the skin, and Pinot Noir forms the basis for Champagne.

While the grape is the beginning of good wine, the qualities of any particular grape may vary considerably depending on such things as soil condition, climate, amount of water and age of the vinestock. A great wine begins with a great grape, but growing a great grape is difficult unless all the growing conditions are optimal, which is rare, even in the ancient wine regions of Europe.

The Wine Regions of New Mexico

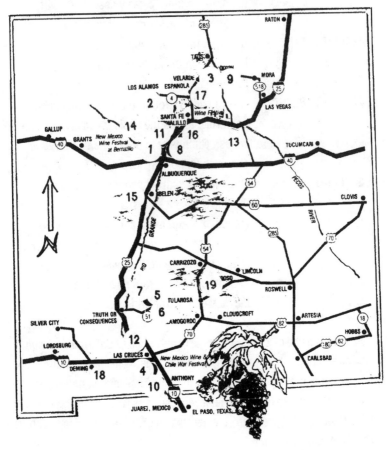

Key to Map:

1. Anderson Valley Vineyards
2. Balagna Winery
3. Black Mesa Winery
4. Blue Teal Vineyards
5. Chateau Sassenage
6. Domaine Cheurlin
7. Duvallay Vineyards
8. Gruet Winery
9. La Chiripada Winery
10. La Viña Winery

11. Las Nutrias Vineyards & Winery
12. Mademoiselle de Santa Fe
13. Madison Vineyards & Winery
14. Ponderosa Valley Vineyards & Winery
15. Sabinal Vineyards
16. Sandia Shadows Vineyards & Winery
17. Santa Fe Vineyards
18. St. Clair Winery
19. Tularosa Vineyards

The Wine Regions Of New Mexico

The vineyards of New Mexico can be divided into three regions: northern, central and southern. Because of climatological differences due mostly to altitude, which determines the amount of precipitation and length of growing season, as a rule, different grapes are grown and different wines are produced in each region.

The vineyards of the northern region are mostly north of Santa Fé tucked into the Sangre de Cristo Mountains (the southern extension of the Colorado Rockies) at altitudes that average about 6,500 feet. Due to the shorter growing season and harsher winters, vintners have favored French hybrids, such as the red Chancellor and Baco Noir, or the white Seyval and Vidal.

The pure vinestocks of Europe, such as Chardonnay and Cabernet, have a rough time surviving in the north and exist only in small pockets, mostly along the Rio Grande, in what are termed micro-climates. Thus, you will find Pinot Noir, Merlot, Sauvignon Blanc and Riesling, among other viniferas, growing in places thought impossible a few years ago.

The central wine growing region is mostly north and to the west of Albuquerque. At an average elevation of 5,000 feet with daytime temperatures about five degrees warmer than in the northern region, the central vineyards have a longer growing season. French-American hybrids are popular while an increasing number of pure vinifera stock has been planted, such as Chardonnay, Zinfandel and Cabernet Sauvignon.

The southern region lies around Las Cruces, fifty miles north of El Paso at an average elevation of 3,500 feet. With sandy loam soil, long summer days of intense heat and cool nights with temperature drops of at least thirty-five degrees, the growing conditions for wine grapes are the most ideal, comparable to those of California's Napa Valley and regions of Europe.

It is in the southern region that the pure European vinifera stock, such as Chenin Blanc, Merlot, Riesling, the Cabernets, Sauvignon Blanc and Zinfandel, do their best.

The southern region also contains the state's three Appellation regions: the middle Rio Grande Valley, roughly from Belen south through Truth or Consequences; the Mesilla Valley, around Las Cruces; and the Mimbres Valley, to the west of Las Cruces around Deming.

In the United States, Appellations are regions loosely designated by the federal government where the grapes grown supposedly share common characteristics. The main purpose of these designations, as in Europe, is marketing, although the standards laid down by the Bureau of Alcohol, Tobacco and Firearms (BATF) are nowhere near as stringent as those of Europe. American winemakers who use grapes from a specified appellation region may advertise that fact on their labels.

Major Wine Grapes Grown In New Mexico

Vinifera Red
Cabernet Sauvignon
Pinot Noir
Merlot
Ruby Cabernet
Cabernet Franc
Zinfandel
Grenache
Brunello
Lemberger
Nebbiolo
Gamay (a Pinot Noir clone)
Sangiovese
Mission
Carignane
Malbec

French-hybrid Red
Baco Noir
de Chaunac
Léon Millot
Chancellor
Maréchal Foch

Vinifera White
Sauvignon Blanc
Riesling
Chardonnay
Muscat Canelli
Chenin Blanc
Gewürztraminer
Pinot Blanc
French Colombard
Thompson Seedless
Sémillon
Viognier

French-hybrid White
Seyval Blanc
Vidal Blanc
Villard
Aurora
Cayuga

How Wine Is Made —
The Basics

Wine can be made from any fruit that contains sugar. The advantage of grapes is the skins contain natural yeasts that react chemically with the sugar (in fermentation) to form alcohol and a by-product, carbon dioxide. With other fruit, apricots, for example, yeast must be added. (Although, cultured yeast is sometimes added to grapes.)

After the grapes are harvested, turning grape juice into wine depends on the skill of the winemaker, even though modern techniques are employed to control every aspect of the process.

The crushed grapes are put into sterilized vats for fermentation and the temperature is carefully controlled. Red wine is fermented at 68-88F; white wine at 50-75F. In New Mexico, sugar may be legally added to ensure the correct alcohol content.

For red wine, the skins are left with the grape pulp for up to three weeks. The skins add color and tannin, a natural preservative that determines the shelf life of the wine. For white wine, the skins are usually removed immediately.

Fermentation may take two weeks or more until most of the sugar has been changed to alcohol or the alcohol level has reached 15% volume. Red wine traditionally is placed in oak casks for up to two years. The length of aging and type of wood affects the final taste. Aging in French oak barrels, for

Appellation D' Origine Controllé

A concept begun in the 1930s by the Frenchman Baron Le Roy of Châteauneuf-du-Pape, the appellation control system in France has developed into a strict production code system wherein virtually every aspect of the winemaking process is scrutinized and regulated. To use the name Champagne, for in-

instance, yields a different taste than American oak. White wine is usually stored in stainless steel vats.

Lastly, the wine is filtered before being bottled and corked. The amount of filtering is yet another variable controlled by the winemaker to develop his individual style.

Wine bottles are typically stored horizontally to keep the cork from drying, a practice usually reserved for longer periods of storage. If the bottle of wine you just purchased is to be opened immediately, 'laying the bottle down,' as it is called, is not necessary.

stance, the winemaker must satisfy all the requirements for the *Champagne* region of northern France. The product must meet standards of alcoholic content, grape yield per acre, method of cultivation, including pruning and vinification, and even how the wine is stored and aged.

Wine produced outside the *Champagne* appellation region must be labeled 'sparkling wine,' produced by the *Champagne* method.

A Few Tips On Tasting Wine

When you visit wineries, proprietors will usually invite you to taste some of their wines. To help you make the most of the moment, here are a few basic wine tasting guidelines. Remember, you are tasting the wine, not drinking it. Do not feel obligated to consume everything in the glass. Receptacles are usually provided for discarded wine and spitting after tasting is not considered bad manners.

- **Taste the white wines first,** as they are generally the lightest, then **finish with the reds,** which are usually heavier.

- **Taste the dry wines before the sweet,** as sweetness deadens the palate.

- Hold the wine against a white tablecloth and **check for color.** Red wines should be a cherry red or slightly darker. A wine that is too light or has a brownish character may have deteriorated.

- **Check for clarity.** Wine should have a brilliant color and be generally free from sediment. Some wine is produced with only a minimum of filtration in which case sediment or residue may appear in the bottom of the bottle (some wine bottles have an indented bottom to trap such sediment).

- Gently **swirl the wine** in the glass to expose it to the air. Put your nose into the glass and **sniff for aroma.** The fermentation of grapes gives the wine a distinct fragrance. A vinegary aroma or a wine that smells like a musty cellar are indications of a poor wine.

- 🍷 Sip a little wine and roll it around in your mouth to **check for flavor.** A bitter taste in red wine is characteristic of excessive tannin. The lack of acidity in whites is often the sign of a poor wine.

- 🍷 **Check for body.** This is the 'weight' of the wine as sensed by your tongue. Red wines tend to feel heavy; white wines tend to feel light.

- 🍷 Lastly, swallow the wine and **check aftertaste,** that is, the wine's crispness, cleanness and overall 'polish.' The flavor and aroma should 'unfold' as it slips down your throat.

A Basic Guide To Serving Wine With Food

The adage, 'red wine with meat, white wine with fish, and rosé for everything,' is a generality at best. Today's broad spectrum of wines allows you to enjoy a full-bodied Chardonnay with a steak or a red wine with seafood.

No longer are there hard and fast rules for pairing wine with food. Much depends on your personal taste and what you like to cook. You will learn as you go by tasting different wines, pairing them with various foods, and thus inventing your own pleasing combinations. To help you get started, here are a few guidelines:

- In general, **choose the food first,** then select the wine to complement it. Remember, you are looking for a marriage between the two; the wine should not overpower the food, nor should the food mask the wine.

- Serve **light** (usually white) **wines with light meals** and full-bodied (often red), **robust wines with hearty meals.**

- Feel free to **contrast a wine** with a particular food. For instance, a sweet Sauternes is excellent with a salty Roquefort cheese. Or, you may **pair a wine with a similar food.** For example, the same Sauternes may be served with a sweet dessert.

- If more than one wine is being served at a meal, the **lightest and simplest wine** should be served **first,** followed by the heavier, more complex wines. **Sweet wines** should be served **last.**

- Consider **how and where** a wine will be served. A picnic or barbecue calls for a light, fruity, easy-drinking wine, while a formal dinner demands a more complex wine.

- The **sauce, seasoning,** and the **cooking method** are more **important** in choosing the right wine than the actual meat or fish being served. For example, a light meat such as chicken might normally be paired with a light, white wine. Chicken in a chile sauce, on the other hand, would demand a fruitier red wine.

- Lastly, an aperitif of **dry wine,** champagne, or chilled, dry sherry, **stimulates** the palate before a meal paired with wine. **Mixed drinks,** especially if they are sweet, **deaden** the palate and make it difficult to savor the dinner wines. Again, follow the guideline of the **lightest and driest wines first; heavy and sweetest wines last.**

With this bit of history behind you and some hints on wine and food to pique your interest, you are ready to tour the wine producing areas of *New Mexico: The Cradle of North American Wine.*

The Northern Winery Tour

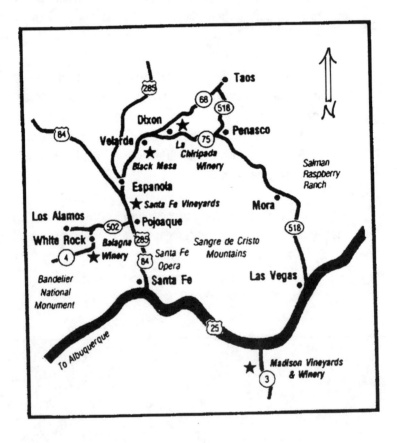

2

LA RUTA DE LAS VIÑAS DE LA REGIÓN DEL NORTE

(The Winery Tour of the Northern Region)

Introduction

Northern New Mexico offers some of the state's most picturesque touring, much of it on winding two-lane highways that weave through traditional Hispanic villages. Against a backdrop of piñon-studded foothills and majestic cottonwoods clustered along the banks of clear mountain streams, you'll explore the ruins of ancient pueblos, retrace a part of the Old Santa Fé Trail, step across a Civil War battlefield and experience the rich diversity created by New Mexico's triad of cultures—Native American, Hispanic and Anglo.

The northern winery tour is a 250 mile, two-or-more day loop through some of the most spectacular scenery and historic regions in the western United States. The first day's drive of about 115 miles begins by heading east out of Santa Fé toward Las Vegas, roughly paralleling the Old Santa Fé Trail, then north along the eastern edge of the *Sangre de Cristo* (Blood of Christ) Mountains to Taos with stops along the way.

After time spent exploring the historic sites of Taos, the second leg of the loop, about 135 miles, heads southwest along the Rio Grande, branches off into the Jemez Mountains, and then loops back into Santa Fé.

The Tour Begins—
The First Day

From Santa Fé (original name: *La Villa Real de Santa Fé de San Francisco de Asís,* the Royal Village of the Holy Faith of St. Francis of Assisi), proceed north on I-25 toward Las Vegas following the route of the historic Santa Fé Trail used by Indians, traders and wagon trains.

(As an option, you may exit south on Highway #285 for Galisteo and the Santa Fe Brewery. This will add about twenty-five miles and a couple of hours to your tour—see the last chapter on New Mexico Microbreweries for details. Otherwise, continue toward Las Vegas).

Enroute to Las Vegas, you will drive through Apache Canyon and over the 7,400 foot elevation, Glorieta Pass. It was near Apache Canyon that the Mexican Governor, Manuel Armijo in 1846, decided not to defend his Mexican colony against the American general, Stephen Kearny, who had already claimed the land to the east, including Las Vegas, as American territory. Armijo retreated south, leaving all of New Mexico to the Americans.

Glorieta Pass was the site of the only major Civil War battle in New Mexico. Union forces out of Colorado and New Mexico met Confederate forces from Texas in a battle known as 'the Gettysburg of the West,' which took place in March of 1862.

Continue north on I-25 to the Pecos exit (#299) and on State Road #50 into

---

Remember Pecos Bill?

Bill was born with all his teeth and red hair. His first words were "Gimme a drink." Bill played dead-eye poker at three, chewed tobacco and brushed his teeth with prickly pear cactus. Crossing the Pecos River as a baby, he fell out of the wagon and grew up in New Mexico playing with coyotes.

Later, when his horse, Widow-Maker, died, young Bill saddled a mountain lion and whipped him into action with a 12-foot rattler. Everybody agreed Pecos Bill was the toughest cowboy in the west. Honest!

the village of Pecos on the banks of the Pecos River. This historic river, which spawned the Pecos Bill of cowboy folklore, winds 1,100 miles out of the glacier-sculpted mountains of northern New Mexico through the west Texas plains into the Rio Grande.

The village of Pecos, founded in 1700, is an old Hispanic community with strong traditions. St. Anthony's, a typical northern New Mexico church with its pitched tin roof and elaborate steeple, looks out over the river from the center of town. The 13,000-foot mountain peaks to the north of Pecos are some of the highest in the state.

Turn right at the 'T' onto State Road #63 and head south toward the Pecos Historical National Park. On your left is Adelos, a funky, old time general store (a gas pump, fishing licenses, bait, canned goods—a look at the old days). The Pecos Ranger Station, on the highway to your right, provides information on the Pecos Wilderness.

Fly Fish The Pecos

Some of the best summer and fall flyfishing in New Mexico is along the Pecos River. The cold waters of this picturesque stream are stocked with trout—rainbows, cut throat, and browns. Hike the river and fish from the bank or wade in over the rocks to a knee-high, brisk current. Cast a mayfly or grasshopper into water so clear you can see the trout waiting. Catch and release. Good for the fish, good for the stream, good for you.

The Pecos National Monument embraces over a thousand years of history. Five hundred years ago the ruins now visible were part of an important trading center situated on the trade route between the Pueblo farmers of the Rio Grande valley and the hunting tribes of the plains to the east. The Pueblo consisted of a large, multilevel apartment complex, four and five stories high with at least 660 rooms and more than 2,000 inhabitants.

With the arrival of the Spanish Franciscan priests in the 1620s, a mission was built at Pecos. The most imposing of all New Mexico mission churches, it was 90-feet wide by 170-feet long, with towers, buttresses and great pine-log beams and high adobe walls. When the Pueblo Indians revolted against the Spanish in 1680, the church was destroyed, but was rebuilt on a smaller scale twelve years later when the Spanish reconquered the land.

Stop first at the visitor center to view a film and exhibits before touring the ruins. During the summer, Native Americans and Hispanics demonstrate traditional crafts.

Upon leaving the park, turn right heading south toward I-25. On the left you will pass several buildings, which constitute the main entrance to the Forked Lightning Ranch, a 13,000-acre cattle ranch once owned by Hollywood legend Greer Garson.

In 1991, Garson sold 5,500 acres to a conservation fund, which donated the land to the Pecos National Park. On both sides of the road you will note the Garson Ranch's signature of blue gates and pink adobe columns ornamented with small lightning bolts.

Back on I-25, head north to exit #323. Turn south on State Road #3, a narrow, winding road that hugs the Pecos River, toward the town of Ribera (Spanish for 'banks,' or 'shore').

Ribera was an important Pecos River crossing for wagon trains on the Santa Fé Trail and was also a Mexican customs station for goods coming from the east coast into Mexican territory.

Hollywood's Mrs. Miniver

Born in 1908, in County Down, Northern Ireland, Garson was discovered by Louis B. Mayer on the London stage. He brought her to Hollywood in 1939. She starred in 25 movies including 'Goodbye Mr. Chips,' 'Pride and Prejudice,' 'Sunrise at Compobello,' (playing Eleanor Roosevelt) and 'Mrs. Miniver,' for which she won the Oscar for best actress in 1942.

Garson played strong, independent women and earned seven Oscar nominations. Married to Col. Buddy Fogelson in 1949, Greer called the Forked Lightning Ranch home until 1992.

A couple of miles further south is the San Miguel national historic district. The church, with its twin towers and three-foot-thick rock walls, measuring twenty-feet high, was built in 1805. Inside is a display of silver donated by parishioners; beneath the floor, prominent members of the community lie buried.

Another two miles and we are at the picturesque Madison Vineyards and Winery, a small, family owned 'boutique' winery on the banks of the rambling Pecos River.

MADISON VINEYARDS & WINERY

Tucked into the bend of the narrow road, opposite red sandstone cliffs that drop sharply to the ground, an ancient cottonwood shades a Hobbitt-like house built of old adobe and stone. Wildflowers bloom by the front door and a handwritten note instructs, 'Please ring bell.'

Beyond, a fertile valley with rows of grapevines spills into the Pecos River. It was here, in 1980, one man planted four acres of vines and taught himself to make award-winning New Mexico wine.

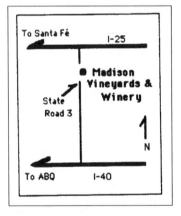

Bill Madison, a bear of a man in his forties, with thick, curly brown hair, a deep voice, and a diamond stud in his right earlobe, admits to having a wild streak. Abandoning the family lumber business in Roswell, New Mexico, he stumbled upon his present property while hunting for artifacts.

"I thought it was the prettiest place I had ever seen," says Bill. "It was once a hippie commune in the '60s. The property went up for sale and I bought it a few years later.

"I had $10,000 and that's what 10 acres and the shell of an old adobe house cost. It caused a divorce and my family was mortified I wouldn't

Bill and Elise Madison's winery is tucked into a Hobbit-like house of adobe and stone ringed with spring flowers on the banks of the Pecos River.

do the lumber yard," he adds. But he persevered, slowly rebuilding and adding on to the old adobe. Providentially perhaps, he discovered a grapevine growing by the old out house.

"Getting into the wine business was a fluke. I knew nothing about it," he admits. "But I kept thinking about that lone vine and wondered if I could grow grapes here."

After talking to some local vintners, he planted a few vines and began selling the harvest to another small winery. "I got my first French hybrids from New York and the Chardonnays and Rieslings from California," he recalls. "I planted eighty the first year. Then Elise came and knocked on my front door."

Elise, now Bill's wife and mother of their two girls, was living in Los Angeles. She had come to New Mexico on a ski trip with a friend who was an acquaintance of Bill's, decided to stay and became Bill's partner. She suggested if they were going to grow grapes, they might as well make the wine, too.

With dark eyes set in a porcelain complexion, Elise usually answers the bell and leads guests through the stone hallway into the living room where a small tasting table stands next to the baby grand piano. She is eloquent in her explanation of wines she and her husband produce.

The two had no previous wine experience and learned from reading every wine book they could lay their hands on. They planted different French hybrids, turned their garage into the winery and used a dilapidated, undersized apple press for their first crushing. It took eighteen hours to crush a mere 200 gallons of juice.

"At first, I was going to do the wine and Elise was going to take care of the books," says Bill. "That soon changed."

"The real key to making wine is blending," he explains. At first I was just pouring things in. Elise watched for a while and said this is not the way to do it. She's a nurse and knows how to mix medicines, and she does that with wine. She has a much finer palate than mine.

"We started out by making the kinds of wine we like to drink, really dry, stark, high acid wines," explains Elise. "However, we began to change when we discovered customers wanted a lower acid, softer wine."

"Folks would come in and say they liked a dry wine and we'd give them one and they didn't like it," adds Bill. "They thought a wine with .75 residual sugar was dry." At that time, the Madisons had no residual sugar in their wines. Now they're moving towards .25 residual sugar.

"Sugar softens the wine, if not making it unperceptively sweeter to the customer," explains Elise. "It's hard for us because we like dry wine better, but we are trying to target all the way through, from dry to sweet. Our newest wine is a Sauvignon Blanc, a blend of Sauvignon Blanc and Aurora, which won a silver medal at the '93 New Mexico State Fair."

A mark of the Madison style is the use of old milk dairy tanks for fermentation. Paddles, which used to keep the milk from separating, slowly rotate inside the tanks giving the fermenting wine a distinct flavor while simultaneously providing refrigeration.

"We ferment in everything," says Bill, including plastic wine tanks and oak barrels. The wine is often available to the public soon after it is bottled, usually the spring after harvesting.

With the addition of a new press, they will have two, two-ton presses to speed the crushing along. Madison produces eight or nine wines a year, translating into 3,800 gallons or 1,600 cases, which they distribute in Santa Fé, Las Vegas and Albuquerque.

"I think we're going to get to the 5,000 gallon stage and then stop," Bill adds. "I don't want any employees."

With four acres planted in Aurora, de Chaunac, Baco Noir, Seyval, and Riesling grapes, the Madisons can handle the winery themselves. The vines are planted in sandy loam soil on a high water table, so they rarely need watering. To complete their grape needs, they buy from growers in Santa Rosa, Belen, Dixon, and Deming

An annual harvest party turns the usual back-breaking work of picking grapes into an enjoyable event under the sun.

"I collect names of people throughout the year who are up for it," says Elise. "The weather is nice, there are conversations across the chin-high vines with new friends, and we have a barbecue outside so everyone can watch the crushing. It's made the picking a little more relaxed."

Still, a winery always has complications, especially at an altitude of nearly 6,000 feet. Two years ago, the vineyard was bombarded with hail just before harvest and all the grapes were lost. Another year, the wine in the fermentation tanks turned to icy slush during an early freeze.

"With wine, the work never ends," says Bill. "If I had known more, I would have planted only one red grape and one white. We still don't do things quite right, but it's very forgiving, and there are always options."

Ten years after their first harvest, the Madison team of two is still exploring those options and producing award-winning wines on the banks of the scenic Pecos River.

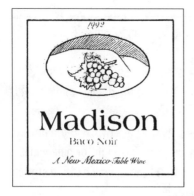

WINES IN PRODUCTION

Sauvignon Blanc or a **Chardonnay** (depending on availability of grapes), **Proprietor's Reserve** (made primarily from a blend of French hybrids—Baco and de Chaunac), **Baco Noir** (A French hybrid), **Pecos Wildflower** (A blend of Riesling, Muscat Canelli and French hybrid, Seyval Blanc),

Desert Rose (A fruity rosé—grapes vary) and **Seyval Blanc** (a white wine using French hybrid grapes).

Elise Madison offers her recipe for Pecos Crab using Madison Vineyards' Pecos Wildflower wine.

Ingredients:
   2-3 cloves of garlic, minced
   1 leek or onion, chopped
   2 Tb. olive oil
   1 Tb. butter
   1/2 lb crab (or imitation crab)
   1 cup snowpeas
   1/2 cup Pecos Wildflower

Sauté garlic and leek or onion in olive oil. Add butter and sauté crab. Add snowpeas and sauté until bright green. Add wine and allow to simmer until alcohol has burned off, about 20 minutes. Serve crab mixture over Udon or Soyba noodles along with a glass of Pecos Wildflower.

Details: Madison Vineyards & Winery. Founded 1980. Star Route 490, Ribera, NM 87560 (505) 421-8028. Winery and Tasting Room open   10-6 every day except Sunday (12-6). Proprietors/Wine makers: Bill & Elise Madison.

Gunfighters Galore

In the 1880s, Las Vegas had the reputation as the most violent of all frontier towns. Twenty-nine men were killed or lynched in one month. Illustrious visitors included Billy the Kid (who complained loudly about the town jail), Doc Holliday (who owned a saloon on Center Street until he killed a drunk in 1880 and ran for Tombstone with his girlfriend, Big Nosed Kate), Bat Masterson, Wyatt Earp, Scar-face Charlie, Web-fingered Billy, and Jesse James (who vacationed at a hot springs north of town).

THE NORTHERN TOUR CONTINUES

Retrace your route to I-25 and head north to the historic town of Las Vegas. The sweeping prairie lands to your right were for centuries the hunting grounds of Comanche Indians who chased immense herds of buffalo, antelope and elk. The buffalo have vanished but herds of elk and antelope remain, sometimes visible from the highway.

Exit #345 into Las Vegas ('the meadows'). Follow University Avenue to Bridge Street and cross the Gallinas River to the old town plaza.

Las Vegas (original name, *Nuestra Señora de los Dolores de Las Vegas,* or Our Lady of Sorrows of the Meadows) was founded in 1835 primarily as a service center for trade along the Santa Fé Trail and as a Mexican port-of-entry until General Kearny proclaimed the town United States territory in 1846. Kearny is said to have read the proclamation from the rooftop of 210-218 Plaza, an act that helped fuel the war with Mexico, which lasted from 1846 to 1848.

Teddy Roosevelt's Roughriders

Nearly half of TR's famous Roughriders were from New Mexico, with Las Vegas their headquarters. Their first reunion in 1899 found Teddy sleeping at the Phoenix Hotel five miles north of town in Montezuma, now home to the Armand Hammer United World College of the American West. The Roughrider Memorial and museum is on Grand Avenue.

With the arrival of the Santa Fe Railroad in the 1870s, Las Vegas became a boomtown of tents and shacks with all the blood and violence typical of frontier society.

Wagon trains loaded with trade goods, wool and flour often stretched for five miles into the plains. Fifty wagons a day waited outside the flour mill to have wheat ground. Half-a-million sheep populated local ranches while the human population only exceeded six thousand.

By 1900, Las Vegas was the largest town in the New Mexico territory (New Mexico became the 47th state in 1912) and monopolized trade for hundreds of miles around, from Albuquerque into southern Colorado and even west Texas.

A walking tour (pick up a guide map from the Chamber of Commerce) of old Las Vegas will reveal a mélange of architectural styles—Pueblo and Hispanic adobe alongside stone and sandstone of the Greek and Gothic Revival period, Victorian, Queen Anne, Romanesque and a half-dozen other motifs from the east.

After lunch, take State Road #518 north out of Las Vegas through *Sapello* to *La Cueva* hugging the Sangre de Cristo mountains on your left. To your right, in the valley below, is the historic route of the Old Santa Fé Trail. (Wagon tracks are still visible to the discerning eye, but you have to know where to look.)

Sapello is a farming community at the confluence of the *Sapello* and *Manuelitas* creeks. To your left is Hermit's Peak, a landmark for wagons on the Santa Fé Trail. The peak was named after an Italian hermit who came from Kansas on the Santa Fé Trail in 1863. He lived in a cave and was said to have performed many miracles, including bringing forth the waters of the creek he drank from. His popularity as a healer drove him from his cave into southern New Mexico where he was murdered in 1869.

At *La Cueva* (Spanish for 'The Cave,' as early residents reportedly lived in nearby caves) is a National Historic District of several mercantile buildings belonging to the 35,000-acre Salman Raspberry Ranch. Owned by David and Marilyn Salman, the ranch features the largest raspberry farm in New Mexico.

Built in the 1870s, the adobe mill, with its 18-foot waterwheel, ground flour for Fort Union, a calvary outpost and supply depot along the Santa Fé Trail, about twelve miles due east. During this period, the local farmers grew so much wheat that the Mora Valley was known as the 'Ukraine of the Southwest.' The mill also generated electricity for the surrounding valley until 1949.

On the rolling green hills behind the mill are the rock wall remnants of buildings and stockades for cattle, sheep and goats. The starkness of the rock walls is softened in the summer by lush wildflower gardens that beckon visitors to take long walks.

In the late 1700s, the Spanish found wild raspberries along the river and named the valley Mora ('berry'). Raspberries have been commercially grown on the Salman Ranch off-and-on since 1930.

Currently, twenty acres of organically grown Heritage variety raspberries produce 15,000 quarts of fresh berries and 20,000 jars of gourmet jam annually, in addition to syrup, vinegar and honey. (All available at the Salman Ranch Store or shipped by mail order throughout the country. For information, (505) 387-2900).

Overlooking the raspberry fields is the big house, or *hacienda*, a two-story rambling building featuring white, ornate ironwork along the second story balcony. It's one of the few examples of Monterey Peninsula Territorial Style architecture in New Mexico.

Built in 1863, the house was surrounded by a high, adobe wall (parts can still be seen). At the approach of danger, a bell would ring and field workers would run for the shelter of the enclosing walls.

Nearby is the San Rafael Mission church, also built in the 1860s. Its thick adobe walls are traditional but its French Gothic windows were in-

Home of Kit Carson

Mountain man, trapper, scout, soldier and Indian agent, Kit Carson arrived in Taos as a teenager in the 1820s. He spent most of his early life in the Rockies guiding trappers and fighting Indians. In 1842, he met explorer John C Frémont and guided Frémont and his men in their exploration of the West.

Carson was one of the first to see Los Angeles in 1846. He fought in the Civil War, pioneered the Santa Fé Trail and helped negotiate treaties with the Navajo, Kiowa and Ute tribes. He died in 1868 and is buried off the Plaza in Kit Carson Park. Carson's Taos home is now the Kit Carson Museum.

spired by early French missionary priests.

At this point we part company with the Santa Fé Trail, which veers northeast through Raton, while we head northwest on State Road #518 toward Mora. Continue through Mora and Holman, climbing the backbone of the Sangre de Cristo Mountains. Shortly beyond Tres Ritos (an old mining camp) is the Sipapu Lodge and Ski Area, the oldest in northern New Mexico. At this point, Taos is just twenty-two miles away.

Continue on State Road #518 into Taos for the night and as many days as you wish.

Taos, (original name, Don Fernando de Taos) is actually three towns, although commercialism has blurred the distinction. The most northern and oldest is the Taos Pueblo; then Taos itself, the commercial center; and Ranchos de Taos, the southern village and site of one of the most photographed and painted of all churches—made famous by Georgia O'Keeffe, Ansel Adams and others— the Ranchos de Taos Church.

Sipapu: The Pueblo Creation Myth

The Pueblo, Apache and Navajo peoples share the vision that this world is but one of several. The present world—the world of light—is the mediator between the earth mother and sky father. The first people were female and were born underground. They migrated up from the underground, layer by layer, in an arduous journey of great anxiety into light.

'Sipapu' is the place of emergence from the underworld into this world, much like a hole in the earth. But, the earth is believed to be only a way-station in the final transcendence to the sky father to reside with the deities of thunder and lightning.

More formally known as the San Francisco de Asís Church, the Ranchos Church was built during the period 1772-1815, and is possibly the finest example of the blend of the Franciscans' Old World architecture and Southwestern building techniques.

The church itself is fortress-like with four-foot thick adobe walls and massive log beams (*vigas*) with fine corbels. The large exterior adobe buttresses seem to root the church into the brown sandy soil giving the entire structure an organic earthiness.

The Taos Pueblo is thought to have been settled eight hundred years ago by a group of Tewa-speaking Indians following an eagle. The Pueblo is considered the center of the Taos Indians' religious activities and has neither electricity nor plumbing. The Taos Pueblo is the purest form of Pueblo architecture and remains the most photographed of all the nineteen existing New Mexico Pueblos.

The Spanish arrived in the early 16th century but the mission was not established until 1598. The general settlement of the Spanish did not happen until nearly twenty years after the 1680 Pueblo revolt, the Spanish having found the Taos valley one of the most difficult areas to reconquer.

A visible remain of the Spanish legacy is the two-hundred-year-old Taos Plaza, historically one of the busiest trading centers in New Mexico. A branch of the Santa Fé Trail passed through Taos introducing goods from the east. At the annual trade fair, the Commanche, Pueblo and Ute Indians laid down their weapons to meet on the Plaza to swap hides, meat, grain, horses and tobacco with Spanish and Anglo traders for tools, guns and cloth.

(One of the current attractions off the Plaza is Eske's Beer Pub, a Taos microbrewery. See the last chapter on New Mexico Microbreweries).

Painting Down The Bones

She was forty-one years old when she traveled alone to Taos from the east in 1930 seeking new vistas for her painting.

Georgia O'Keeffe was stunned by the stark beauty of the mountains and the thin, dry air that played tricks with the light. "No one told me it was like this," she said.

When the artist returned home, she carried a suitcase of bones and skulls, items to inspire her creative spirit.

Fifteen years later, in 1945, O'Keeffe purchased a run-down, northern New

Reportedly by 1846, several million dollars worth of furs and pelts changed hands annually rivaling St. Louis and Vancouver as one of the most important fur markets in the country. That Taos might some day emerge as an art community was little in the thought of these early traders. It was not until the 1880s, with the arrival of artists Bert Phillips and Ernest Blumenschein that a new chapter of Taos' history would be written.

Both men found themselves stranded outside Taos when one of their wagon wheels broke. By the time they fixed it, the two had fallen in love with the Taos valley and began what became known as the Taos School of Art, a style that depicted the Southwest through romantic lenses and helped spark the myth that endures, in part, as the 'Santa Fé Style.'

Mexico hacienda near Abiquiu on the Chama River.

She furnished her new home with the bones, shells, pine cones, driftwood and feathers collected on her walks, to be the subjects of many of her famous paintings. O'Keeffe died in 1986 at age 98.

To the artists attracted to northern New Mexico, the turquoise and violet sunsets against the earthen colors of the land and the white, puffy clouds that floated as sailing ships across unbroken horizons overwhelmed the more unromantic aspects of life on the frontier: the extreme poverty of the Pueblo peoples and diseases such as tuberculoses.

It was not, however, until the arrival in 1917 of a wealthy eastern woman, Mabel Dodge, that the reputation of Taos as an art colony began to spread. A colorful figure, Mabel became the center of a constant flow of artists including Andrew Dasburg, Georgia O'Keeffe, Ansel Adams and D. H. Lawrence.

THE TOUR CONTINUES — THE SECOND DAY

After breakfast, leave Taos on Highway #68 heading south toward Española. The road climbs and winds around the foothills as the highway moves closer to the Rio Grande. Soon the road enters the Rio Grande canyon and the highway and river share what little space is available at the bottom of the canyon.

This stretch is a favorite of canoeists, river rafters, fishermen and picnickers. Where bottom land is available, you will see small farms and orchards. Groves of ancient cottonwoods line the often muddy waters. The town of Pilar (named after a famous shrine in Spain) was once a Jicarilla Apache farming community that was sacked by the Spanish in 1694.

At State Road #75, turn left for two miles following the Rio Embudo (Embudo River) to the town of Dixon and La Chiripada Winery, which is through town on the left.

LA CHIRIPADA WINERY

When the Johnson brothers, Mike and Pat, bought a small tract of land called La Chiripada ('stroke of luck' in Spanish) in northern New Mexico in the late '70s, they had no idea how well it would suit their new venture.

Tucked into the narrow but fertile Rio Embudo valley amid a patchwork of apple orchards and artist's studios, alongside the Embudo River with its plentiful supply of trout, is the town of Dixon and the oldest winery in the northern part of the state.

The Johnsons planted their first French hybrid vines in 1977, and opened their picturesque handbuilt adobe winery a few years later. Now, surrounded by ten acres of robust vines, the winery is a well established feature of the northern New Mexico landscape.

"It's satisfying to make something with your own hands and have somebody buy it and appreciate it," says Pat, in his shy, understated way. A potter turned winemaker, Pat was joined by his two other brothers, Mike, who provided the inspiration for the winery from his early experiences in California vineyards while studying to be a Jesuit priest, and Mark, a cabinet maker and carpenter who designed the winery.

Pat's wife, Michelle, designed the wine labels. She was using traditional Mimbres figures, animals drawn by the Mimbres Indians, on her pottery and decided to incorporate them into the wine labels to express the regionality of the wine.

While Mark eventually left to pursue other ventures, the 'Chiripada Boys,' as Mike and Pat became known, stayed on to produce award-winning wines. Mike attributes their success to their sense of taste and skill at blending.

"Blending is probably one of our strongest points as winemakers," says Mike. "To be a good winemaker, you have to have a palate. Wine blending is a dialogue, a creative tension between different palates. We understand that, and there's a lot of give and take between us. You have to try to open up when you're tasting wines and not be locked in by expectations.

"Basically, we like to accentuate the fruit qualities in the grape. However, our Chardonnay and barrel-select white do accentuate some vinification methods like oak-aging and barrel fermentation. We try to marry the fruit quality with the vinification process. All our reds are oak-aged for anywhere between twelve and eighteen months in a combination of French and American oak casks."

They believe in a minimum of movement and filtering of the wine. "Everytime you do a process like fining or filtering or even pumping, you're taking something out of the wine," adds Mike.

Born in Southern California, Mike and Pat grew up in Colorado and New Mexico before settling back into California's Santa Clara Valley where they worked for Paul Masson on sparkling wine (Champagne) production. Pat eventually became a potter and in the early '70s, Mike joined the Jesuit order in Los Gatos, California, where he spent ten years, but was not ordained.

"That's where I was introduced to grape growing and wine drinking," says Mike. "The Jesuits had vineyards at the time and made Muscat, sherry, and altar wine from Palomino grapes."

Mike Johnson, one of the "Chiripada Boys," hand corks a bottle of their award-winning Rio Embudo Red.

In 1977, the brothers were drawn back to the beauty of northern New Mexico where Pat and his wife, Michelle, made and sold their pottery. On the side, Pat and Mike started an experimental winery with one hundred French hybrids because of their hardiness in sub-freezing temperatures.

By the next year, they had planted 600 more vines including Léon Millot (a hybrid crossing of an American vine with Goldriesling used in their Rio Embudo Red), de Chaunac, and Seyval Blanc. Later, they added Vidal Blanc, Siegfried Riesling, and two varietals, White Riesling and Chardonnay.

Over the next six years, they would plant another 6,500 vines in the canyon, a valley of flat, sloping plains with well-drained sandy loam soil.

"We have about 7,000 vines now, planted close together, European style, with about ten acres under cultivation, five of which belongs to a neighbor. That supplies nearly sixty tons a year, or roughly half of what we need," says Mike. "The other thirty tons are bought from other vineyards in the state.

"Virtually all our pruning, watering, fertilization and netting (to keep the birds away) are oriented towards our cold climate. So, we prune late, figure out when to fertilize, and how to water. Basically it's flood irrigation from the *acequias* (ditch canals) in the canyon that were developed in the late 1600s by the Spanish.

"Pat and I always felt the wine industry in New Mexico ought to accent a regional approach. There is a tendency to copy California. Find grapes that grow well here and make good New Mexico wines. The regional grape for New Mexico would have been what they call the Mission grape, but that is inferior. The French hybrids work well and I think we've developed a regional wine for northern New Mexico.

"Winemaking is very simple in a way," adds Mike. "But we're aggressive about taking care of the wine. During the aging process we lose 5% from evaporation from the oak barrels. Every two weeks we have to 'top off' the barrels to keep them full. If you do everything right you should end up with pretty decent wine.

"Well, I've never worked on a wine so hard as our Chardonnay," interrupts Pat, "to make it a drinkable wine." Mike nods his head. "But the style went over real well. We're thinking of making it a little heavier next time, more oak."

La Chiripada utilizes mostly Italian equipment, high grade plastic tanks for storage, and French and American oak barrels for the Chardonnay barrel select and all the reds. Everything is done by hand, including the bottling and corking. The brothers produce about 3,000 cases a year, which they distribute themselves within the state and ship to loyal out-of-state customers who have discovered their wines on trips to New Mexico.

"We don't want to expand. As it is, Pat and I can handle it, with a couple of helpers. But if I had the time, I would like to plant some Rhône valley vines, Spanish or Italian varieties, in the southern part of the state. I think they would do fine. But who has the time?" he shrugs, with a wink and a smile.

WINES IN PRODUCTION

Chardonnay (usually made from 100% Chardonnay but marketed as 'Winemaker's Select White' to allow for blending with other wine, such as Vidal), **Rio Embudo White** (made from Seyval Blanc French hybrid grapes), **Rio Embudo Red** (a blend of 60% Léon Millot and 40% de Chaunac, Silver Medal San Francisco Wine Competition).

(The Rio Embudo wines (white and red) are the signature wines of the winery and prime examples of northern New Mexico regional wines. Rio Embudo Red was also mentioned favorably by Bon Appetit magazine in an article on southwestern wines.)

Primavera (a blend of Riesling and French hybrids, Vidal and Villard. Served at the Santa Fe School of Cooking), **Sonrojo** ('to blush' in Spanish. A blend of Aurora Blanc, red Cascades and Rosettes grapes), **Vintner's Reserve Red** (a blend of Chancellor, Léon Millot and Ruby Cabernet), Port (made from Léon Millot grapes, not brandy fortified) and **Apple wine** (a blend of Stamen, Winesap, Delicious and Jonathon apples, all native to northern New Mexico, when available).

🍷🍷🍷

Details: La Chiripada Winery. Founded 1977. Box 192, Dixon, NM 87527 (505) 579-4437. Winery & Tasting Room open 10-5 year round except Sunday. Off-site tasting room on the Plaza in Taos, open 10-5 daily. Proprietors/Wine makers: Pat & Mike Johnson.

THE TOUR CONTINUES

Dixon is part of the apple growing region of northern New Mexico and has also become an artist's community. The first weekend in November hosts the annual Dixon Studio Tour, a cooperative venture by twenty-five members of the community ranging from furniture makers, jewelers and potters to La Chiripada Winery and the El Bosque Garlic Farm. Many members have studios open year round.

Retrace your route on State Road #75 back to Highway #68. Turn left (south) toward Velarde. On the right you will pass Embudo Station, ('Embudo' means funnel) where the river rushes through the high walls of the gorge. This is the site of the Embudo Gauging Station used to measure the flow of the Rio Grande.

On the level field across the river is the remains of the old Denver and Rio Grande Western Railroad station, a leftover from the 1880s when agricultural goods were transported out of the valley to Española and further south. Currently, a restaurant occupies the site. In the summer tables are spread under the arching limbs of the cottonwoods. A pleasant meal can be ordered as the river quietly moves by at your feet.

After lunch, visit the Embudo Station Microbrewery behind the restaurant (See the last chapter on New Mexico Microbreweries).

Continue south on Highway #68. As you emerge from the canyon the river broadens and slows, and continues in this fashion for most of its remaining journey through New Mexico. At this spot in 1696, Don

Diego de Vargas defeated the Taos Indians to finally squelch the Pueblo Indian uprising of 1680.

Six miles further south is the town of Velarde. This part of the Rio Grande valley is an agricultural center featuring apple and peach orchards. It is also the home to Black Mesa Winery, one of the newest of Northern New Mexico's boutique wineries.

BLACK MESA WINERY

Maverick vintner Gary Anderson isn't easily discouraged when it comes to making his own style of wine. When a university professor said vinifera grapes could not be grown on his land, a thirteen-acre tract

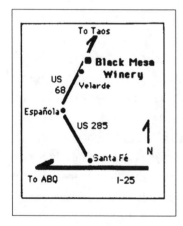

across from the Black Mesa at the mouth of the Rio Grande canyon, Gary grew them anyway.

When others warned of the dire consequences of blending viniferas with hybrids, he thought it worth trying.

When the Bureau of Alcohol, Tobacco and Firearms informed him that each barrel had to be numbered for tracking, Gary gave them names instead.

"Numbers are boring," says Gary. "Names, especially family names, are OK." To the reds he gave male names: Oliver, Merle, Peter, Tom ("Isn't Oliver a great name for a barrel?" Gary asks, rhetorically); to the whites, female: Sondra, Darlene, Joyce, Penny.

An orthopedic surgeon by training, Gary and his wife Connie started as amateur wine makers in the early '70s in Denver, Colorado. They always dreamed of opening a winery as a retirement project some day. While on a three-month sabbatical at the labs in Los Alamos working in the laser department, they stumbled upon a parcel of land in Velarde. With sloping canyon walls and a southeastern exposure, it seemed destined for growing grapes.

Red chile ristras *embrace the entrance to Black Mesa Winery, one of northern New Mexico's newest boutique wineries.*

After some debate, Gary took early retirement and they moved to New Mexico, although he continues a part-time practice in Taos, which has helped to underwrite the winery equipment.

Nothing had been planted on their land before, although Velarde had once been thickly planted with grapevines, even as recently as the 1940s. The soil is what is known as the Santa Fé Formation, the same clay and loamy sand from which adobe bricks are made. When a government man suggested apples would do better, the vines were ripped out and apples planted.

'We weren't encouraged by people, so we knew a vineyard would be a struggle," says Gary philosophically. "Consequently, we didn't mold our operation after the advice of the local wine people. We just wanted to make a good wine, and hopefully, a unique wine. That's when we decided to try vinifera-hybrid blends."

Not knowing what to expect, his first vines were planted on an experimental basis. Pleased with the results, Anderson has planted all his land in grapes: a mixture of reds (Léon Millot, Lemberger, Merlot, Pinot Noir, Cabernet Franc, Shiraz), and some Chardonnay. He even has vines planted on the steep slopes of the canyon wall behind the winery among boulders ornamented with petroglyphs four hundred to two thousand years old.

The vines on the slope are on drip irrigation until the roots establish themselves deep enough to find water. "We're using head and trellis pruning systems, now," says Anderson. "As we go on, we'll probably prune more to a colder climate, called fan pruning, which is not well known except in this area. This allows several stalks instead of one, to fan up from the base.

"The grapes that have done very well are the Lemberger (no relation to the cheese, Limburger)," says Connie. "They're a German red vinifera from the Prosser area of eastern Washington. Their climate is quite similar to ours, so we thought the plants should transfer well."

By spring of 1994, the Andersons expect to have at least 1,000 vines under cultivation, although they won't be yielding wine-caliber grapes for several years. The first harvest is typically when the plants are five years old. " But it is well known," says Gary, "that eight and ten- year-old vines are better than five-year-old vines." Certainly, in establishing a vineyard, patience is a virtue.

Until the plants mature, however, Black Mesa will continue buying grapes from other vineyards. Because Gary has a winer's license (as opposed to the more common grape grower's license), he can use out-of-state grapes in his blends, although he tries for local grapes whenever possible.

"We use California grapes primarily for our signature wine, Coyote," says Gary. "The blend began exclusively with California grapes but has since been altered. Now, the major grape is the New Mexico Chancellor, a French-hybrid from the Rhône area. We blend it with Grenache, another commonly grown grape in the Rhône area, and Valdepeñas, a Zinfandel-like vinifera (a Spanish-style Cabernet). The last two are only available in California.

"Our philosophy is to try to produce something that tastes more like earth than fruit, and that means longer in the barrel," he explains.

To get that earthy taste, Gary believes in filtering as little as possible. The by-product is sediment, but he's trying to educate the consumer to decant, that is, to pour the wine from the bottle into another container, leaving the sediment behind.

Gary is proudest of his 'big reds' that have been fermenting in small oak barrels, particularly the Antelope Cabernet and a straight Baco Noir.

"Baco is to New Mexico what Cabernet Sauvignon is to Bordeaux," says Gary of this French hybrid grape that grows so well in the northern part of the state. He also likes the Léon Millot, calling it a real sleeper.

"We were involved with a group called 'the grape nuts,' he says. "There were six of us. We decided to put some money together and taste the world's finest wines to see if there was indeed a difference. There was a difference, but the value wasn't there. In the process, we learned a few secrets."

Some of those secrets are shared in the wines produced by Gary and Connie Anderson, the 'grape nuts' of Black Mesa.

WINES IN PRODUCTION

Wood-Nymph Riesling, Solstice Riesling (with a higher sugar content than the Wood-Nymph), **Seyval** and **Vidal** (French hybrids), Coyote (a Rhône-style red wine that is a blend of Chancellor, Grenache and Valdepeñas. The signature wine of Black Mesa), **Hollyberry Nouveau** (a red wine made from American Beta grapes and Léon Millot), **Aleman-Rojo** ('German Red.' Made from Lemberger grapes imported from eastern Washington), **Chardonnay**, **Cabernet Sauvignon**, and a St. Emilion style of Cabernet Franc Merlot.

Connie Anderson suggests pairing Black Mesa Aleman-Rojo with her recipe for Gruyére-Garlic Puffs.

Ingredients:

1/4 lb butter	4 eggs
1 cup hot water	1/2 cup grated Gruyére cheese
1 cup flour	4 cloves finely chopped garlic
1/4 teaspoon salt	Roasted garlic cloves

Melt butter in the hot water in a sauce pan. Add flour and salt all at once. Cook until mixture is smooth and forms a soft ball that does not separate. Remove from heat, cool slightly and add eggs one at a time beating vigorously after each egg is added.

Add cheese and garlic bits. (Garlic must be very finely chopped, not pressed or smashed.) Drop batter onto greased cookie sheet using not much more than one teaspoon of batter. Bake in hot oven (375-425) for

15-20 minutes until golden. One may roast garlic cloves to insert into the small puffs, or serve plain.

🍷🍷🍷

Details: Black Mesa Winery. Founded 1991. 1502 Highway 68, (Box 432) Velarde, NM 87582. 1-800-852-MESA. Winery & Tasting Room open 10-6 year around except Sunday. Proprietors/Wine makers: Gerhard (Gary) & Connie Anderson.

THE TOUR CONTINUES

Continue south toward Española on Highway #68. The town of Española (original name, *San Gabriel de Los Españoles)* lies on the banks of the Rio Grande and serves as the commercial center of Rio Arriba County.

At the first stop light after entering Española, turn right, go to the next light, about half-a-mile, and turn left. You are now on the Los Alamos highway. Follow the signs to Los Alamos. Veer to the right at the downtown 'Y' (still in Española) onto State Road #30. Eventually, on #30 you will pass the Santa Clara Pueblo.

The Tewa-speaking peoples of the Pueblo moved south from Colorado perhaps a thousand years ago. The explorer Coronado reported seeing the Pueblo in its present location when he passed through in 1540. The Franciscans established a mission in 1622. The Pueblo controls over 40,000 acres of rich farmland and historically

Lowrider Capital, USA

On Friday and Saturday evenings Española is bumper-to-bumper with customized 'low and slow, mean and clean' cars known as 'lowriders.' Lethargically, they creep up and down the city's arteries at snail-pace speeds, their undercarriages only inches above the ground.

A carryover from So. California of the '50s, these cars are brightly painted in metallic colors, and sport welded, chrome chain steering wheels, crushed velvet interiors and hydraulic lifters enabling the autos to rise and fall on their axles. A long line of lowriders is great fun to watch.

has been self-supporting in agriculture, although many work at Los Alamos, Española and in Santa Fé.

The Pueblo is most noted for its black pottery and for the Puye Cliff Dwellings, dating from 1450, which are carved into the face of the Pajarito Plateau. These dwellings were the first of the Rio Grande ruins to be systematically excavated and represent some of the most extensive early American cliff villages in existence. Unlike many ruins, which are national monuments, the Puye ruins remain under the control of the Santa Clara Pueblo.

Visitors to the Pueblo may visit the Puye ruins but otherwise are generally limited to the Plaza of the Pueblo itself unless permission is obtained from the administration building, or during festivals open to the public.

Continue past the Pueblo on State Road #30 until the road melds with Highway #502.

Follow the signs to White Rock (which is adjacent to Los Alamos, the world renowned scientific complex that developed the Atomic Bomb) on State Road #4, home of Balagna Winery perched on the edge of the magnificent White Rock Canyon.

Upon reaching White Rock, continue to the first stop light. Three roads past the stop light, turn left onto Monterey, which connects with Rio Bravo Drive. Balagna winery is at 223 Rio Bravo Drive. The tasting room is generally open daily from 1-6 pm. (As this winery is somewhat out of the way, you may wish to confirm it is open to visitors by phoning 672-3678. The view alone is worth the effort.)

BALAGNA WINERY

When a retired nuclear chemist from Los Alamos decided to commemorate the 50th anniversary of the atomic bomb by releasing a red wine called 'La Bomba Grande,' in 1993, he didn't know just how much controversy it would cause or how popular the wine would become.

"I thought I might be able to sell a few as a novelty," says winemaker John Balagna. So he blended 50% Zinfandel with 25% Pinot softened with 25% Merlot and designed a 'killer' label: the mushroom cloud of the trinity shot (the first A-bomb test in southern New Mexico in 1943). "I had a little difficulty getting the Bureau of Alcohol, Tobacco and Firearms to approve the label," John chuckles. "The BATF has to approve every wine label in the country. Finally, I received permission on the third try by adding, 'For Sale Only in New Mexico' at the bottom of the label.

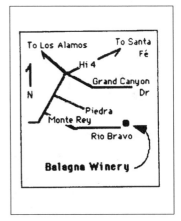

John can't sell La Bomba Grande out-of-state, but that doesn't keep friends in Los Alamos from shipping cases to their friends.

"It's been a great hit, if I overlook complaints I've gotten from the anti-nuclear community. I even had a write-up in Newsweek. Several cases have gone to Russian scientists as gifts. They loved it."

Balagna's Italian, 'politically incorrect' sense of humor carries over to another label: 'Dago Red.' Half Chancellor, a hybrid red, and half Vidal, a French hybrid white, Dago Red is a smooth, simple table wine that accounts for one-third of his sales.

'Dago' was a derogatory name given to early Italian immigrants. During Prohibition, a private citizen could legally make 200 gallons of wine for personal use. Every Italian began making their own in the garage, their cellar or attic.

"To most southern Europeans," John explains, "wine is a food to be consumed with a meal. Before long, simple red table wines came to be called 'Dago Red.' It could be anything, any red wine.

"My family was always making cellar wine," as he describes it. "My grandparents emigrated from Italy but I grew up in Colorado. Every fall, my dad would ship in three or four carloads of grapes from California to sell to people in the coal camps so they could make their own wine. I guess making wine kind of comes naturally.

"Back in '59, I planted French hybrid grapes behind my house. They did pretty well but it's so damn cold up here, I never ripened a grape. This is tough country for grape growing." Balagna now buys all his grapes from growers down south.

Balagna Winery opened commercially in 1986. He built a wine tasting room on the rim of White Rock Canyon. As you kibitz with the winemaker and taste the fruits of his labor, the Rio Grande winds silently by hundreds of feet below. About 60% of the winery's annual production of a thousand cases is sold at the tasting room.

Like all good vintners, John has his own style of wine making.

"After I crush the whites, I let the juice sit on the skins for a day or so to extract more flavor. My 'Celeste' white wine, I think, is unique in the state for that sweet reserve added back.

"On reds, I use the old Italian method of leaving the juice on skins until the cap sinks. This means the alcohol level is as high as it's going to get and will no longer support the skins, so they sink. This doesn't happen for six-to-eight weeks, so I've extracted a lot more flavor and color out of skins than if I'd fermented for only a week on the skins, like many wine makers."

John points out the old Coca Cola syrup barrels he uses for fermentation. He also uses old dairy tanks with built-in coolers. Instead of oak barrels, Balagna employs 'medium toast' oak chips from barrel builders in Napa. He drops the chips in a barrel for about a month. After three weeks he begins to taste. When he has enough oak flavor, out come the chips.

"My chemistry background has helped," John concedes. "There's a reasonable amount of chemistry to do." What's the key to good wine? "Cleanliness. That's the first thing. You've got to start with good grapes and you've got to know what you're doing."

Balagna thinks New Mexico grapes stack up beautifully against the competition. "We have such nice growing weather and we don't have mold problems like they do in California.

"If someone's not too familiar with wine," he counsels, "they'll usually go for the sweet whites. Aficionados will head for the hearty reds. I'm trying to develop a good Zinfandel. But the best Zinfandel comes from Amador County in California where the vineyards are 150 years old. Zins don't really begin to develop until you get twenty or twenty-five-year-old vines.

"I'm also thinking of a new robust red wine with the label: New Mexico Red Wine—Not for Wimps."

WINES IN PRODUCTION

Chardonnay, Riesling, Celeste Blanco ('Heavenly White,' half Riesling and half French hybrid Seyval), **Dago Red** (a blend of Chancellor and French hybrid Vidal, considered the signature wine of Balagna Winery), **Zinfandel, Pinot Noir** and **La Bomba Grande** (a blend of Zinfandel, Pinot and Merlot—The wine that won John Balagna national recognition).

IL SANTO CELLARS

New Mexico Table Wine
DAGO RED
CONTAINS SULFITES

PRODUCED AND BOTTLED BY
BALAGNA WINERY, LOS ALAMOS, NEW MEXICO
NM-BW-50

Details: Balagna Winery. Founded 1986. 223 Rio Bravo Drive, Los Alamos, NM 87544 (505) 672-3678. Winery & Tasting Room open daily, 1-6 pm   Proprietor/Wine maker: John Balagna.

THE TOUR CONTINUES

After leaving the Balagna Winery, backtrack on State Road #4 past the cutoff for Los Alamos, perhaps the most famous scientific community in the world for its work on nuclear energy, particle physics, nuclear chemistry, radiobiology and computer science research. The Laboratory, which boasts one of the highest concentration of Ph.D.s in the country, is also home to GenBank, the international data base for DNA genetic research.

Follow State Road #4 until it turns into the four-lane Highway #502, and head toward Santa Fé. Enroute, you will pass the San Ildefonso Pueblo, a reservation of 26,000 acres with only a few hundred inhabitants, but the home to one of the greatest of all Indian potters, the late Maria Martinez, noted for her black-on-black technique.

Highway #502 connects with Highway #285 at Pojoaque. Veer left for Española and continue on Highway #285 for three miles to Santa Fe Vineyards on the right.

SANTA FE VINEYARDS

Len Rosingana developed Santa Fe Vineyards as a personal challenge. Could northern New Mexico support a profitable winery? Could he produce New Mexico wines that would find an audience?

Previously, in California in 1975, Len along with his brother, Harry, had founded Stoney Ridge Winery and were soon producing 50,000 cases a year on a shoestring budget.

"We were doing some innovative winemaking," Len recalls, "such as bottling White Zinfandel before it became a household wine and producing Pinot Noir from Monterey grapes."

Several years later, when he married a Santa Fé native and they decided to move back to Santa Fé, Rosingana brought wine making equipment with him from a California winery and decided to experiment with what he could do in New Mexico. The result was Santa Fe Vineyards, a winery that has grown from the first year's production of 200 cases in 1982, to 6,500 cases in '93, all the winery can handle at its present location.

Of Italian descent, Rosingana remembers his grandparents' tradition of

Project exploded its first Atomic Bomb at Trinity Site in the desert of southern New Mexico. For ten years after the end of WWII, Los Alamos was still a tightly guarded secret only going public in 1957.

winemaking brought with them when they emigrated to America from the Piedmont region of Italy. Two generations later, one of their grandson's wines, Blanc de blancs, a blend of white French hybrids, would be served at the inaugural luncheon of George Bush.

The winery is in a constant flurry of noisy activity. The size of a small warehouse, it is packed with several 1,500-gallon stainless steel fermenting tanks and a row of American oak barrels. Pumps and hoses snake across the cement floor and in the middle of the chaos, an automated machine fills, corks, capsules and labels the winery's latest production.

Rosingana has elected not to grow his own grapes, but has focused his business exclusively on making wine.

"A few years ago, in the early '80s," he says, "I planted six acres of vines close to Cerrillos on the river. It was virgin land, good soil, but the water was brackish. The vines were infested with bugs, then the neighbor's cows broke in. It was just too difficult. I was better off buying grapes."

Len remembers all-too-well the early days of making wine in Santa Fé. "Just finding grapes was difficult," he recalls of the early '80s. "I've probably bought grapes from every vineyard there is in New Mexico."

Though still tenuous, the supply has gotten more stable in recent years with the large vineyards in the southern part of the state.

He orders his grapes custom picked, crushed, and chilled so he can pick up the juice the following morning. Back at the winery, he immediately begins the fermenting process, usually putting the reds outside in a refrigerated trailer and the whites inside in stainless steel tanks.

Space is limited for fermentation in oak, but he does age some Cabernet Sauvignon and Chardonnay in American oak barrels from Missouri, that lend a toasty, spicy flavor as well as character to the wine. He bottles the wines as they are ready and produces ten to twelve different labels each year, mostly varietals and a few hybrid blends.

"My skill is in the making of the wine and pulling out as much from the grape as I can. From there it's a matter of bringing it up to the caliber I want," he says. "I've got pretty high standards of what I want to put out."

Rosingana refines his taste from the 400 wines he samples each year from Italy, France and the United States and looks for wines that appeal to a broad spectrum of people.

"I want wine to taste like a Chardonnay if it's Chardonnay," he explains. "Obviously, there will be some different attributes coming from New Mexico. There's not enough vineyards to draw from to be able to take distinct essentials and put them together like you do in California. We have several talented people here producing grapes but we don't yet have the broad spectrum California has."

For example, both his Chardonnay and Cabernet are a blend of varietals from two different vineyards. "That's all that's out there," he explains. "One vineyard is usually big and full-bodied and robust while the other's a little lighter and more flowery and you put the percentage together."

Another aspect of New Mexico wines is their relatively short shelf-life. For the most part, they are not meant to be laid in a cellar but enjoyed, especially the whites and blush wines. That's usually not a problem for most Americans, who generally drink wine within twenty-four hours of purchase.

"They just don't seem to have more than one-and-a-half years worth of life," says Rosingana. "The Cabernet you could lay down for two to three years, but no more than five." He attributes this short life to the fact that New Mexico's grapes are not yet fully mature.

"In California, the better Chardonnay comes after the fifteenth year of growth. We're in our eleventh or twelfth year in New Mexico. You're just not going to see it yet and you may not see it until the vines have had twenty years growth. It's going to depend on how well we're dealing with the land."

One of the most recognizable assets of Santa Fé Vineyards are the labels designed by Armado Maurillio Peña, Jr., a mestizo of Chicano Yaqui heritage. The winery's first label was a colorful and detailed design of a vineyard stretching out to a Zia sun flanked by two Indians.

"We met Peña through a friend and now he's married to my sister-in-law," explains Rosingana, who commissioned Peña to do the label for the winery. "It was so popular we had him design another label of three Indian women with pots for our Indian Market White."

The labels were another smart business move that has placed Len Rosingana and Santa Fe Vineyards on the viticultural map of New Mexico.

WINES IN PRODUCTION

Santa Fe Vineyards

New Mexico White Table Wine
Indian Market White

Viña del Sol (a blend of Sauvignon Blanc, Chenin Blanc, Semillon and French hybrid Seyval), **Sauvignon Blanc, Chardonnay, Indian Market White** (made from Muscat Canelli), **White Zinfandel, Santa Fe Blush** (a blend of white wines with Cabernet Sauvignon for color), **Tinto del Sol** (a blend of Ruby Cabernet, Cabernet Franc and Merlot), **Cabernet Sauvignon,** and **Merlot.**

Details: Santa Fe Vineyards. Founded 1982. Box 216A, Espanola, NM 87532 Phone/Fax (505) 753-8100. Winery & Tasting Room open 10-5 Daily. Proprietor/Wine maker: Len Rosingana.

THE TOUR CONCLUDES

Return to Santa Fé heading south on Highway #285. On your right, approximately six miles north of Santa Fé, you will pass the Santa Fé Opera.

Singing To The Stars

Music critics laughed at a summer opera company. No one would come, they said. Opera stars went to Europe for summer festivals. Who had heard of Santa Fé, anyway?

John Crosby, a young opera impresario, ignored the jibes. He recruited Igor Stravin-sky to personally supervise 'The Rake's Progress' for the opening season. That was in 1956.

Today, the Santa Fé Opera is the premier summer opera festival in the U.S. The Opera has trained an entire generation of world-class singers, including Samuel Ramey, Kiri Te Kanawa, Alan Titus and Frederica von Stade. It's a popular place to be on a balmy, star-studded August night. But book ahead!

High on a hill, surrounded by tall, shimmering poplar tress, the 1,700-seat theater is located in a natural bowl tucked into the hills on the site of the old San Juan Ranch House. The theater is a soaring structure, partly covered, partly open to the night sky with admirable acoustics and a loyal international following of opera enthusiasts who flock to Santa Fé for the July/August season.

Continue past the Opera turnoff on Highway #285 and follow signs to the historic Santa Fé Plaza, the traditional end of the Santa Fé Trail arriving from Missouri and *El Camino Real*, from Mexico City.

The Plaza, in constant use for more than four hundred years, was once the geographical center of Santa Fé. It was much larger in Spanish times and served as a large outdoor market for traders and Indians. During the Mexican period, up to 1848, the Plaza contained a bullring, which was eventually destroyed as it provided shelter for marauding Indians. At the beginning of the American period it was reduced to its present size, enclosed with a white picket fence and often planted in alfalfa.

Along with the fence, the Americans constructed two story adobe structures on the three sides of the Plaza facing the Palace of the Governors, which was built in 1609 as part of the Spanish royal presidio, or military headquarters. The Palace of the Governors is the oldest public building in continuous use in the United States.

During most days of the year the portal of the Palace is filled with Indian jewelers and potters selling their creations. In the center of the Plaza is a monument erected by citizens after the Civil War. Close study of the monument's inscription will reveal references to both rebels and savages, although the word 'savages' was chiseled out many years ago by an unknown person.

A second marker, explaining the historical context of the Civil War monument, has been placed nearby as the result of an agreement among the nineteen Pueblos, the Navajos, the Apaches and the city.

Today, the Santa Fé Plaza is perhaps the most famous of all the Spanish-inspired plazas, certainly in the United States, and hosts a variety of cultural activities including the annual world-famous Indian Market, held over a long weekend each August.

> ### Indian Market
>
> International collectors of Native American art make a pilgrimage each summer to Santa Fé for Indian Market. Held over a long weekend each August since 1921, more than 800 Indian artists participate in the largest juried exhibit and sale of Indian artwork in the country. Strict standards of authenticity are maintained for handmade pottery, baskets, kachina figures, jewelry, drums, sculpture and paintings.
>
> (Information (505) 983-5220)

It is at the Plaza in Santa Fé, steeped in four hundred years of Southwest history, that our Northern Tour ends.

The Central Winery Tour

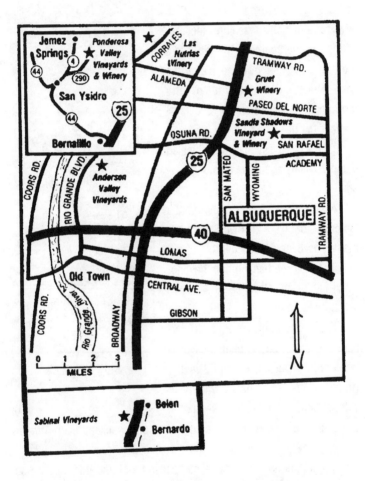

3

LA RUTA DE LAS VIÑAS
DE LA REGIÓN CENTRAL

(The Winery Tour of the Central Region)

INTRODUCTION

From the shadows of the Sandia Mountains, along the banks of the languid Rio Grande with its ancient groves of cottonwoods and family farms, then northwest into the red rock canyons at the base of the Jemez Mountains, the central wine tour is a one day, predominantly suburban tour of about 125 miles. Of the five wineries you will visit, several are claiming national recognition for the quality of their wines.

Our sixth stop, Sabinal Vineyards, is not a winery, but New Mexico's largest organic vineyard producing table grapes and a variety of grape, apple and cherry juices. Sabinal is located about forty-five miles south of Albuquerque near Bosqué. It may be included in the central tour, or may be a stopping point on the way south to Truth or Consequences and Las Cruces, the focus of our southern tour.

The tour begins at Albuquerque's Old Town Plaza, proceeds north on I-25 paralleling the base of the Sandia Mountains to Sandia Shadows Vineyard & Winery, then on to Gruet and their imposing new winery and visitor's center before heading into the red rock canyons northwest of Bernalillo to the pastoral setting of Ponderosa Valley Vineyards and their rustic, tin-roofed winery.

From Ponderosa, the tour winds down the west side of the Rio Grande through the village of Corrales, one of the oldest wine producing regions of New Mexico, to visit Las Nutrias Winery. Continuing south, we cross to the east side of the river to our last Albuquerque stop, the Anderson Valley Vineyards and Winery at *Los Ranchos de Albuquerque.*

From Anderson, you may complete the tour where you began at the Old Town Plaza, approximately five miles further south on Rio Grande Blvd., or take I-25 south through Albuquerque to Belen and Sabinal Vineyards.

Luminarias Light The Way

Early Hispanic settlers used to light small fires of piñon logs along the road to warm themselves on the way to Christmas Eve mass. One tradition claims the fires lit the way for the Christ child. Today, Old Town is aglow at Christmas with thousands of candles set in small paper bags (*luminarias,* or *farolitos,* as they are sometime called) creating a spectacular and moving spiritual vision.

THE TOUR BEGINS

We begin at Albuquerque's historic Old Town Plaza close to the banks of the Rio Grande, which has been the crossroads of the Southwest for nearly three centuries.

The *villa* (or village) of Albuquerque (original name: *Villa de San Felipe de Alburquerque)* was established in 1706 by don Francisco Cuervo y Valdes and thirty families of colonists who had been given permission by King Felipe V of Spain to establish an agricultural center and military outpost along *El Camino Real,* on the banks of the 'Great River.'

Seventy years later, at the time of the Declaration of Independence in 1776, Albuquerque's population was recorded at 763. One hundred-seventy years later, at the end of World War II, the city was still in its infancy, with a population of little more than four thousand. Since then, Albuquerque has exploded with a greater population today of about 480,000, nearly one-third of the state's residents.

Early on, Albuquerque took the shape of a traditional Spanish *villa*, with a central plaza surrounded by a church, government buildings and adobe houses, all designed to withstand Indian attacks.

The church of San Felipe de Neri, now situated on the north side of the plaza, was initially built on the west side but was moved in 1793. Enlarged and remodeled several times over the years, its thick, original adobe mud walls remain intact. The landmark structure still serves the community as a focus for religious life.

In 1846, U.S. General Stephen Kearny proclaimed Old Town part of the United States and established a military garrison. During the Civil War, in 1862, the Plaza was occupied by Confederate forces who left after two weeks without firing a shot.

Do You Remember Kearny?

General Stephen Watts Kearny, that is. In 1846, at the beginning of the Mexican War, Kearny was sent by President James K. Polk in a carefully designed campaign to wrest the New Mexico territory from Mexico. The General was amazingly successful, overcoming most Mexican opposition without firing a shot.

In 1851, the boundaries with Texas were laid and New Mexico became a U.S. Territory until 1912, when it was finally admitted to the Union as the forty-seventh state.

Old Town remained the hub of wagon train commerce until the railroad arrived in Albuquerque in 1880. Thereafter, business gradually shifted to New Town (currently the center of downtown marked by high-rise buildings) to take advantage of this faster and more economical form of transportation.

Leave Old Town heading north on Rio Grande Blvd. Enter I-40 heading east toward the Sandia Mountains. You may exit north on 12th Street for the Indian Pueblo Cultural Center, a large complex owned and operated by the nineteen Pueblo Tribes of New Mexico.

At the intersection of I-40 and I-25, head north toward Santa Fé about five miles, exiting at Paseo del Norte. Continue on Paseo east toward the mountains for about 3-1/2 miles turning right on Eubank. Continue on Eubank for 1/2 mile, and turn left on Coronado. Sandia Shadows Vineyard and Winery is on your right.

Pueblo Indian Cultural Center

Indians were the first settlers of New Mexico, their history predating recorded time. The Pueblo Indians are decendants of the Anasazi, or 'the Ancient Ones.'

Today, there are nineteen Pueblos along the Rio Grande from the Taos Pueblo, north of Taos, to the Isleta Pueblo, south of Albuquerque, with a combined population of over 30,000.

The Cultural Center features traditional Pueblo Indian dances, arts and crafts, native foods and other special events showcasing the cultural heritage of these early peoples.

SANDIA SHADOWS VINEYARD & WINERY

Nestled at the shadowy base of the purple Sandia Mountains in an area increasingly ringed with expensive homes lies the tranquil, thirteen-acre vineyard planted with Sauvignon Blanc, Chardonnay, and Seyval grapes and the winery of Philippe and Sylvia Littot.

A Frenchman with ten years experience in the New Mexico wine industry, Philippe moved to Albuquerque in 1993 from southern New Mexico where he had been overseeing grape production for the French owners of Chateau Sassenage.

Philippe and his wife, Sylvia, a New Mexico native, assumed control of Sandia Shadows, a winery established in 1984, with the intent of producing a French-style wine. Hand-picking the grapes fifteen days early makes all the difference between a French-and-American-style wine, according to Philippe.

"A French-style wine is fresh and crisp, retaining the primary flavor of the grape," he explains. "For myself, American wines don't have this freshness. American-style wine has a powerful aroma, but overall is less distinctive."

For example, the Fumé Blanc, which Philippe considers one of his signature wines, exhibits a nose of both fruit and wood, rather than being heavily covered with oak. His Cabernet is also distinctive.

"My Cabernet, made like French-style wine, and aged like a French wine is completely different," he says. "A good Cabernet must be strong and light, heavy in flavor but light when you drink it. You have to be more professional to appreciate this style wine."

Born in Tunisia, Philippe studied in Burgundy, France, and has a six-year degree in Oenology (the study of wine) from the University of Dijon. He came to New Mexico in the early '80s after several years of winemaking experience in North Africa and France.

"My brother-in-law is in the wine business in Côtes du Rhône," says Philippe. "My father makes wine in Aix en Provence and another brother harvests grapes in Corsica."

In 1987, he returned to France for a few months before being lured back as wine maker at Domaine Cordier Winery in Ft. Stockton, Texas. Soon, he was back at Chateau Sassenage in Truth or Consequences, NM.

Philippe prefers that Sandia Shadows remain a small winery with a goal of 2,000 cases per year, which he distributes himself from the winery. Having watched other wineries go under, he is cautious when it comes to expanding and buying more and bigger equipment. He would rather crush grapes in a single, old-fashioned press and age the juice in French and American oak barrels.

"We grow, pick, and crush grapes by hand," says Philippe. "We do everything by hand. I prefer to work day and night for fifteen days but not to spend any money on nice press machines. That's what everybody does. They say they need a bigger press. For what? Fifteen days a year? You have so much invested for one month and when you use it—when you need it—the machine breaks. Crazy!"

Philippe's hands-on experience in New Mexico during the industry's renaissance in the '80s has been sobering. "We found out it was more difficult to grow grapes in New Mexico at the beginning," he says. "We learned a lot. At the time, there was no state research or university system to draw on. Time and money were spent waiting in the desert for equipment to arrive from California. Not a problem anymore."

Critical to a vineyard's success was understanding the micro-climate of the immediate area. "We did make some mistakes," Philippe admits, "but we didn't know until we made them. In New Mexico it doesn't matter if you are north or south, it is the elevation that is important."

For example, Chardonnay grows extremely well at Sandia Shadows on the slopes of the Sandia Mountains. Yet, just ten miles away down in the valley by the river, the cold weather makes it nearly impossible for Chardonnay to survive. "Sauvignon Blanc here is beautiful. I never saw so many nice Sauvignon Blanc. You go south and they have all the trouble in the world."

Unlike some other wine makers, he does not feel limited by his choice of grapes in the state. "You can make a good wine from the hybrids," he says, holding up his Sandia Nouveau as a prime example. Made from 100% French hybrid Chancellor grapes, it is a Beaujolais-style wine with a rich cherry nose.

He has seen the industry grow up during his years in the Southwest. "Ten years ago, you found only bad wine in New Mexico, you couldn't even drink it," he says. He credits the French with bringing wine making skills to the state. "Now, even in the smallest winery, you find good wine."

He believes his wines, for $6-$9 a bottle, are as good as what the Golden State offers. "We know we are making good wine," he says. "You have to make better wines than California to be in the restaurants."

Philippe is thrilled to have a winery in New Mexico. "You can't imagine the competition you have in wine production in Europe. My family is very happy I am here. In France there is a winery every ten miles," he says. "Here, it's an open market, which is difficult, too. We take a little more time but we are sure we are going to make it."

WINES IN PRODUCTION

Sandia Nouveau (French hybrid Chancellor grapes), **Apple Wine** (a blend of Golden Delicious and Granny Smith Apples), **Coronado's Gold** (a blend of Golden Muscat and French hybrid Seyval), **Autumn Gold** (a blend of French hybrid Seyval, Chardonnay and Muscat), **Sandia Blush** (made from Chardonnay, Chancellor and French hybrid Seyval Blanc). **Fumé Blanc** (Sauvignon Blanc grapes aged in French oak. The signature wine of Sandia Shadows), **Cabernet Sauvignon** (recommended by the Southwest Internacional Wine & Food Review), **Vin de L'Orangerie** (made from Sauvignon Blanc grapes and orange rinds) and **Sauvignon Blanc**.

Philippe Littot offers one of his favorite recipes for *Les Oeufs a la Meurette*, a classic dish from the Burgundy region of France.

Ingredients:

2 bottles Sandia Nouveau	2 quarts water
1 cup olive oil	1/2 pound onion, minced
1/2 pound garlic cloves	1/4 pound parsley, finely chopped
15 basil leaves	12-24 eggs
Salt and pepper to taste	

In a large pot, add all ingredients except eggs and bring to a boil. Lower heat and allow to simmer for 15-20 minutes, until alcohol has evaporated.

Break an egg into the bowl of a spoon and gently dip it in the sauce. Hold the egg in the spoon until the egg has begun to cook. When hard, drop the egg into the sauce. Repeat with each egg. Cook very gently for 25-30 minutes.

Serve with escargots, or fresh pasta with a sauce of olive oil, fresh basil, garlic and onions. Enjoy a glass of Sandia Nouveau during preparation and with your meal.

Details: Sandia Shadows Vineyard & Winery. Founded 1984. 11704 Coronado NE, Albuquerque, NM 87122. (505) 856-1006. Winery & Tasting Room open 12-6 pm, Wednesday-Sunday, year round, or by appointment. Proprietors/Wine makers: Philippe & Sylvia Littot.

THE TOUR CONTINUES

Upon leaving the winery, turn left on Coronado and retrace your steps on Eubank to Paseo del Norte. At this point, you have two choices. If you are interested in riding the Sandia Tramway, billed as the longest span in North America, turn right on Paseo and travel a short way to Tramway Road. Turn left and proceed about a mile until you see the tramway sign on your right.

Three Miles Of Sky-High Travel

Billed as North America's longest aerial tramway, the Sandia Peak Tramway lifts passengers nearly three miles diagonally and almost a mile vertically to the 10,378 foot peak of the Sandia ('watermelon' in Spanish) Mountains in the Cibola National Forest.

The Forest Service observation deck affords an 11,000 square mile panoramic view of Albuquerque and of Mount Taylor, sixty miles distant on the western horizon, one of the Navajo people's most sacred mountains.

If you wish to continue on the wine tour, turn left on Paseo and head back to the Interstate and to our next winery, Gruet.

Gruet is located on the east side of I-25 along the frontage road between Paseo del Norte and Alameda. To find Gruet, do not get back on the Interstate, but head north along the frontage road for about one-half mile. The imposing Gruet Winery building is an obvious landmark.

GRUET WINERY

When Frenchman Laurent Gruet introduced his New Mexico sparkling wine to New Yorkers in 1991, he remembers them joking it must be made of cactus juice. But after one taste, they were impressed by how similar it tasted to French champagne. Today, New York is Gruet's largest out-of-state market for sparkling wine.

A tall, handsome man with curly hair, Laurent seems too young to be producing excellent New Mexico sparkling wine using the *Méthode Champenoise*, (all Champagne not produced in the Champagne region of France must, by law, be labeled as sparkling wine, although it may be produced using the Champagne method.) But, since founding this family-owned winery in 1987, he has created an impressive record.

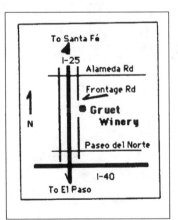

Each year he has striven to improve quality, an imperative to successfully compete against the California producers. Laurent abhors low-end sparkling wine that is chemically produced and responsible for many consumers thinking Champagne causes headaches. He is determined to change the American consumer's image of his favorite beverage.

"I would rather drink a good beer than a cheap champagne," he says. "I know a good beer won't hurt me."

Laurent also wants to correct the misconception that champagne is only for special occasions. "In France, we enjoy Champagne throughout

In the old days, inverted bottles of Champagne were turned by hand, a process called "riddling," to force sediment to accumulate in the neck of the bottle.

the entire meal," he explains, "although you must have red wine with cheese."

His family's half-century of producing Champagne in France has given Gruet a nose for what produces a superb glass of effervescent wine. "The bubbles have to be tiny and stay in the glass, the smell has to be clean and the taste has to be fresh and delicate," he says.

The same high French standards are applied to Gruet's New Mexico sparkling wine with award-winning results. The Gruet label is known as a quality wine at a relatively reasonable price in thirteen states, from New York to Hawaii.

"We try to do wine in the French-style," emphasizes Laurent. "And at a lower price." Even he admits French Champagne is getting too expensive.

Laurent Gruet worked alongside his father for five years producing Champagne in the family winery, Gruet & Fils, just outside Épernay in the Champagne district of France. When they decided to expand in 1980, the cost of land was prohibitive.

Following the success of other French wineries, they looked to the United States. California had too many wineries already making sparkling wine, and Texas weather was too hot for white grapes. New Mexico, however, proved ideal with its high altitude, cool nights, warm days and a consistent, dry climate.

Laurent and his brother-in-law, Farid Himeur, commuted between France and New Mexico for several years until 1986, when, according to Laurent, "we decided to move here forever."

After one more year and much experimentation, they opened their winery, a 2,000-square foot rented warehouse producing 2,000 cases of sparkling wine made from their first harvest of New Mexico grapes. The wine would not appear on the market until late '89, after twenty-four months of aging. Each successive year saw an increase in production until in 1993, a large winery with a tasting room was built to accommodate their current annual production of 18,000 cases.

Gruet buys its grapes from two growers in the south. "Pinot Noir and Chardonnay are the only grapes we use in Champagne, and the only grapes with which to make sparkling wine," stresses Laurent. His contracts with the growers stipulates that he controls the pruning, irrigation and hand-harvesting of the grapes.

Once picked, Farid inspects the grapes before they are loaded into a refrigerated truck. At the winery, entire clusters of grapes are dropped into a mammoth, computerized crusher that delicately extracts the juice by the gentle pressure of a membrane, releasing clear juice known as the *cuvée*.

After three weeks of fermentation and six-to-seven months in the tank, the wine is filtered, yeast and sugar are added, and the wine continues to ferment in the bottle. Gruet sparkling wines are aged a minimum of twenty-four months; the vintages for thirty-six months. "This gives a finesse, complexity and richness to the wine," explains Laurent.

To separate the sediment from the wine, the bottles are put into computerized bins programmed to turn every six hours, forcing the sediment into the neck of the bottle. In the first three years of operation, the wine was stored in a wooden rack and Laurent periodically turned each bottle the old fashioned way, by hand, in a process called 'riddling'.

"All the big Champagne houses in France use computers now, although they keep the wooden racks out front for tourists," smiles Laurent. The machines are more precise requiring only twelve days to complete the riddling process, where the hand method required a month.

When all the sediment has accumulated, the neck is frozen, capturing the sediment in an ice cube. The caps are popped and the force of the champagne blows out the frozen cube. Sugar is added, a process called *dossage*, then the bottles are corked and aged for three more months before being released.

In 1991, Gruet began producing its first still wine, a Chardonnay. Barrel-fermented in French oak for ten months, the result is a delicate, crisp, French-style Chardonnay. Laurent hopes to increase total production of sparkling wine and Chardonnay to 25,000 cases annually by the end of the century.

"When you have a winery, it's a lifelong commitment. You have to love what you're doing and love wine because a winery is a lot of work," he says.

Laurent Gruet is very pleased with the grapes in New Mexico, but wishes Americans would drink more wine.

"In France, people drink ten times more wine than here. If people here drank wine with every meal, I think that would be good," concludes Laurent, with a hint of a smile.

WINES IN PRODUCTION

Gruet specializes in sparkling wines, *Méthode Champenoise*, and produces one Chardonnay.

Brut (made from a 75:25 blend of Chardonnay and Pinot Noir); **Blanc de Noirs** (a 75:25 blend of Pinot Noir and Chardonnay, winner of double gold medals at the San Francisco Fair against 36 sparkling wines from California); **Blanc de Blancs** (1990 Vintage, produced from 100% Chardonnay grapes and aged on yeast for three years. The signature wine of Gruet).

Gruet sparkling wines have been mentioned favorably in Robert Parker's, *Wine Buyer's Guide*, 3rd Ed.

Domaine St. Vincent (Gruet's second label, meant to compete with Spanish sparkling wines);

Chardonnay (barrel-fermented 100% chardonnay grages.

According to Laurent, Gruet sparkling wines (Champagne) may be served for more than special occasions: Serve Gruet as an aperitif before dinner, with appetizers, or any light food such as fish. Sparkling wine is also excellent when paired with lightly spiced foods.

Champagne is often served at weddings or anniversaries along with cake. But, as Laurent points out, this is a mistake as the sweetness of cake overwhelms the delicate nature of Champagne. Better to eat the cake, have a drink of water, and then drink the Champagne.

♈ ♈ ♈

Hot Air Rises

It started back in 1972, when sixteen balloons gathered in one spot for a local celebration. Today, the Albuquerque Balloon Fiesta is an international affair attracting over half-a-million spectators, a national TV audience, and more than 600 balloons and their intrepid crews from around the world.

The most famous event of the Fiesta is the mass ascension. At dawn on Saturday and Sunday of both weekends, wave after wave of glowing canopies float from the ground to meet the rising sun, a photographer's dream. The Fiesta is usually scheduled the second weekend of every October when the high mountain air is clean and bright and the winds are manageable.

Details: Gruet Winery. Founded 1987. 8400 Pan American Frwy, NE. Albuquerque, NM 87113. (505) 821-0055. FAX: (505) 857-0066. Tasting Room open daily from 10-5 pm (Sunday 12-5). Tours available. Proprietors: Laurent Gruet & Farid Himeur. Wine maker: Laurent Gruet.

THE TOUR CONTINUES

As you step from the Gruet Winery, look across the Interstate to the west. Though not visible to the eye, behind the trees are several acres of open field and the home of the Albuquerque International Balloon Fiesta. The event is held ten days each fall in the park located on West Alameda between Edith and Jefferson Streets.

Our next stop is Ponderosa Valley Vineyards and Winery.

Leaving Gruet, return to I-25 and head north toward Bernalillo, about ten miles. Exit the Interstate at Bernalillo (exit #242) to Highway #44 heading northwest toward Cuba and Farmington.

Bernalillo was founded around 1695 as an important trading center due to its location at the northern end of the Sandias and at the confluence of the

80

Jemez River and the Rio Grande. For several hundred years prior to the arrival of the Spanish, Bernalillo was the site of a number of Tewa speaking Pueblos. Reportedly, several Pueblos contained at least 1,200 rooms and as many as a thousand people. Occasionally, pottery shards are still uncovered in and around Bernalillo that date from before the thirteenth century.

When the Spanish explorer Coronado and his troops made their way into New Mexico in 1540, they wintered at Bernalillo and claimed all the nearby Tewa villages as part of Spain's Tiguex Province. Later, in the seventeenth century, large haciendas occupied both sides of the Rio Grande and many of the fields were planted in vineyards.

As you leave town the Coronado State Monument is on the right. Staffed by the Museum of New Mexico, the monument has a visitor's center, museum and a stunning view of the muddy Rio Grande against the Sandia Mountains.

Continue on Highway #44 northwest toward San Ysidro. En route, you will pass the Santa Ana Pueblo on your right. An active farm community, the Pueblo has come back from near extinction at the turn of the century to number more than 500 residents.

Farther along is the Zia Pueblo, which has stood in its present location since the 1600s. The ancestors of the Pueblo's 600 residents are thought to come from Chaco Canyon and Mesa Verde in Colorado. Historically a farming community, the peoples of Zia find jobs off-reservation but are still well known for their beautifully decorated pottery.

The Pueblo is probably best known, however, for their Zia sun, adopted as the official symbol of the state of New Mexico. This ubiquitous symbol—a round circle with four bars radiating to the four points of the compass—adorns the state flag, license plates and can be seen everywhere, from T-shirts to tourist's souvenirs, much to the distress of the Zia people who consider their sign sacred.

At San Ysidro, named after the patron saint of New Mexico's farmers, St. Isidore, we turn right onto State Road #4 for the Jemez Pueblo, about six miles distant.

State Road #4 follows the narrow, winding route of the Jemez River as it cuts through canyons of brilliant colors toward the Pueblo of Jemez. This Pueblo is one of the largest, with a population of about two thousand. Much of everyday Pueblo life can be seen from the car as you pass through the village. (As with all New Mexico Pueblos, tourists are forbidden to take pictures. The Jemez Pueblo, however, encourages visitors to tour their *Walatewa* visitor's center, located in the Pueblo.)

During the summer and fall the road is lined with the brush-roofed lean-tos (*ramadas*) under which Jemez women sell their Indian bread, cookies, pies and crafts to tourists. A number of Jemez Indians are famous artists, writers and potters.

(A good representation of the crafts of Jemez, as well as those of the other eighteen pueblos can be viewed and purchased at the Pueblo Indian Cultural Center in Albuquerque, mentioned earlier in the tour.)

Just past the Pueblo is the turnoff to Ponderosa Valley Vineyards & Winery on State Road #290. Three miles after the turnoff, in a narrow valley, the vineyards appear on your left, with the rustic wood and metal-roofed winery set against a backdrop of a red-rocked mesa.

PONDEROSA VALLEY VINEYARDS & WINERY

When another northern New Mexico wine maker won numerous awards two years running using Ponderosa Valley's Riesling grapes, vineyard owner Henry Street knew he had a winning varietal on his hands. It was so good in fact, the other wine maker encouraged Street to start his own winery. Henry did, and now has to buy grapes from others to meet the demand.

Ponderosa Valley produces three estate-bottled Rieslings and has released a Pinot Noir and Cabernet. But the vineyard owner turned wine maker is committed to doing what works best in New Mexico. So in addition to Rieslings, he produces an apple wine made from four varieties of New Mexico apples, and a french hybrid wine called *Vino de Pata,* loosely translated as 'made with your feet,' a Spanish colloquialism for homemade wine.

"I was always interested in growing grapes, but had only grown them in my backyard," says Street.

When Henry and his wife Mary purchased three acres in the Ponderosa Valley as a camping retreat, they soon discovered numerous small vineyards in the valley, some dating to 1890. The families who owned these vineyards had strong traditions of home wine making. The idea of a vineyard of their own had been planted.

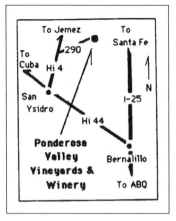

Henry took a course on grape-growing, then researched viticultural techniques around the world to determine what would grow on his land. At the time, he was told by academics that viniferas wouldn't make it, but Street proved them wrong.

In 1976, on the advice of a California wine maker, Henry was encouraged to try Rieslings. Cuttings from a vineyard in California's Livermore Valley were planted at Ponderosa. When these proved successful, additional Riesling cuttings were obtained from Jim Wenty's Monterey Peninsula Vineyards to expand the Street's Ponderosa vineyard to its present size.

Henry then hand-selected from the University of California at Davis' mother vineyard a cold-hardy clone of Pinot Noir that grows in the Gamay Beaujolais style with its cane straight up in the air, similar to that of a Riesling.

"Because we have fall rains, we'd have problems with bunch rot if those grapes grew where they sheltered the clusters," says Street.

By 1978, he was experimenting with a little bit of everything.

"I did a paper study first trying to figure out what would grow. I'm an engineer at Sandia National Laboratory in Albuquerque, so I do things somewhat methodically," he says. "I gave the grapes away to anybody

Henry Street of Ponderosa Valley Winery periodically samples wine from the cask to ensure it is aging well.

who was a good wine maker and would enter the wine in the state fair and give me some idea of what was the best grape to grow here."

After La Chiripada's Special Reserve Riesling walked away with all the awards, the Streets started working with the Johnson brothers. Over the next ten years, they developed a winning style for Ponderosa's Riesling grapes.

A lot of the original vines, like Chardonnay and Gewürztraminer, proved commercially unfeasible and are now gone. In the end, Henry selected varieties that bud only after the first week of May, thus avoiding the inevitable April frosts.

White Riesling and a Riesling clone from southern Germany called Siegfried proved to be best suited to the area and now account for 75% of their plantings, followed by Pinot Noir and a handful of hybrids. Most of Ponderosa's root stock is ten to twelve years old and fully matured.

"They grow better Chardonnay at lower elevation, but up here we grow very good Riesling and incredibly fruity Pinot Noir," says Henry. "By September it has cooled down and the process of maturity has slowed down, giving the grapes a longer period to develop their true character."

Because the harvest is late, birds are not a threat and bugs are minimal. The well-drained, volcanic ash soil is naturally rich in micro-nutrients, requiring only fertilization ('pomace,' the organic waste left over from the wine process, does the trick).

In the fall of 1993, Ponderosa did their first bottling, 480 cases, while they were building the winery. "We had no idea what we were getting into, so we wanted to start small," explains Mary. By Christmas that same year, they were sold out.

The small, 1,800-case winery reflects the Streets' desire for a func-tional operation. The crush deck holds stainless fermentation tanks on wheels, a stemmer-crusher, and old Italian basket presses. "I like the Italian presses because they are real gentle on the wine," says Henry.

The 500-gallon stainless tanks were originally used by an Albu-querque laundry to distill water. "Everything in this place is used, there's nothing new," he says.

For cold fermentation, he simply rolls the fermenting tanks into the walk-in refrigerator, kept at 55 degrees.

Cold-stabilization is handled naturally in the 'cold room,' purposely left open to the elements. The wine is pumped into tanks and kept until the temperature drops below freezing for two weeks, usually in mid-December.

"I don't want to filter the wine more than I have to and that's twice at the absolute maximum. With the cold temperatures, the wines clarify themselves," says Henry.

After filtering, the wine is gravity fed down a tube into the cellar where Henry and Mary bottle, cork and label each batch by hand. A dumbwaiter lifts the cases up to the tasting room where most of the wine is sold. Mary, who wears a name tag proclaiming herself CEO, runs the tasting room. Several restaurants in the area carry the Ponderosa wine as well as a select few wine shops in Albuquerque. The remaining cases are sold at state wine festivals.

The winery's current production is 1,000 cases, but the Streets are looking for an increase to 1,800 cases in the future. In spite of the growth, they plan to remain uniquely New Mexican.

"I can't do California and I can't do France and hope to ever make it because the wine would come across as fake. I want to be New Mexican. I'm after a wine style that is dictated by the grapes we grow; wine that has its own unique character but still pairs well with food," says Henry.

"I know we make excellent Rieslings here. I got a bronze medal for my first attempt. It's my style and I live or die by that, meaning I sell them or I don't. And we haven't had any problem selling them."

WINES IN PRODUCTION

The signature wines of Ponderosa are its Rieslings.

Riesling Dry; New Mexico Riesling (made in the classic German-style with the grapes left on the vine three to four weeks longer than for the Riesling Dry); **Late Harvest New Mexico Riesling** (a sweeter wine made from the last harvest of the Riesling grape, usually in early November when the sugar content is at its peak); **Summer Sage** (a blend of Riesling, Golden Muscat and two French hybrids, Vidal and Villard).

Del Valle Apple Wine (made with Golden Delicious apples. Low in alcohol and not overly sweet); **Pinot Noir** (made in the Gamay Beaujolais style); **Vintner's Red** (made from Cabernet Sauvignon grapes. Should be laid down); and, **Vino de Pata** (a dark red, semi-sweet wine made with Léon Millot grapes in the tradition of early Spanish home-made wine).

Mary and Henry Street offer the following recipe for Drinking Rabbit, made with Ponderosa Vidal Blanc.

Ingredients:

1 large rabbit (3 lbs) cut up	4 Tbs olive oil
2 cloves garlic peeled and sliced	2 onions peeled and sliced
3 Tbs flour	1 sprig fresh rosemary
Salt and pepper to taste	1 cup Ponderosa Vidal Blanc

Sauté the cut up rabbit in olive oil in a heavy dutch oven until brown, about 10 minutes. Add the garlic and onions and cook until soft, another 10 minutes. Stir in the flour, salt, pepper and rosemary. Add the wine, bring to a simmer, cover and place in a 350 degree oven for 45 minutes. Serve with freshly made biscuits and wine jelly, a fresh green garden salad and a glass of well chilled Ponderosa Vidal Blanc.

Details: Ponderosa Valley Vineyards & Winery. Founded 1976. 3171 Highway 290, Ponderosa, NM 87044. (505) 834-7487 or 294-6217.

Tasting room open 10-5 pm Tues-Sat. Closed January. Proprietor and Wine maker: Henry K. Street.

THE TOUR CONTINUES

After visiting the winery, retrace your steps back through the Jemez Pueblo to State Highway #44 and head southeast toward Bernalillo. Just prior to entering town, turn right on State Road #528 and head south toward the village of Corrales and Las Nutrias Vineyard & Winery.

In about five miles you will turn left at an intersection onto Corrales Road (State Road #448).

The village of Corrales ('corrals' in Spanish), is stretched out along the west bank of the Rio Grande for over five miles. The name was derived from the numerous corrals used for sheep and cows to segregate them from the open fields of vineyards and orchards planted in the rich bottomland soil.

Early Spanish, French and Italian settlers have given Corrales a unique European flavor and influenced the early planting of vineyards in this village by the river. Nineteenth-century visitors spoke of the wines, delicious fruits, and wide variety of foods served in local homes. By the 1870s, the area around Corrales was at the center of the state's wine production only to die out during Prohibition.

As you enter the village you will see a sign on the right for the historic old San Ysidro church, about one-half mile off the road. The twin-steepled, tin-roofed adobe building was constructed in the 1860s and is now home to the Adobe Theater, a

The Saint Goes Marching In

In May, at the beginning of the planting season in many northern parts of New Mexico, a statue of St. Isidore, the farmer, is carried through the streets of farming villages and into the fields. Wearing his traditional blue coat and pants, red vest, and a hat with a flat crown, the saint is accompanied by a small angel and a team of oxen. In New Mexico, when it comes to ensuring a good harvest, even the saints are put to work.

Corrales landmark. Las Nutrias winery is shortly after the church on your right.

LAS NUTRIAS VINEYARD & WINERY

"When I started my vineyard in 1982, nobody told me about pruning grapes," Ken laments. "I thought, once-in-awhile. But every year? I had no idea I had to cut them every year. Nobody told me about the bugs. This is virgin soil, I was told. No bugs here. Not true."

Ken Kendzierski, owner and wine maker at Las Nutrias Winery, situated alongside the narrow, tree-lined road that winds through the picturesque village of Corrales, shakes his head and emits a deep throated laugh as he recounts his own innocence about wine making.

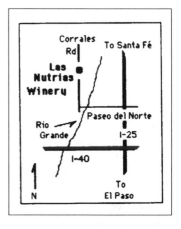

"Every year I have to prune, fertilize and spray for bugs. And we have to irrigate. I had to buy water rights, another expense nobody told me about. In the growing season we irrigate twenty-four hours a day, non-stop, and then we hope the April frost doesn't hit us like it did in '93. In 1992, we had 160 tons of grapes; a year later, we had forty tons."

Ken moved to New Mexico in 1970 from Delaware, where he had been working for a chemical company. He was on his way to Long Beach, California, for a job in the space industry, stopped for a few days in Albuquerque and never left.

Enamored with the wine industry from his travels in Europe after college, Ken bought one hundred acres of virgin land near the small village of Las Nutrias ('The Beavers' in Spanish), about sixty miles south of Albuquerque, and planted thirty acres of French hybrids—Seyval, Vidal and Chancellor—on contract for another winery.

In the meantime, Ken had planted an additional thirty acres of viniferas—Chardonnay, Riesling and Pinot—because, as Ken tells it, "I had been misinformed as to the grapes I should have planted."

The winery Ken was supplying abruptly folded leaving him with tons of grapes ripening each fall. He had to find an outlet, so he applied for his own winery license and began making wine.

"Our first vintage was 1985, which I still have," said Ken, with a hearty laugh. "That's how bad it was."

Still, Ken claims that New Mexico produces some of the finest grapes in the world. "We have unique soil and a unique climate. We have more sun than just about any other place. We're not too hot, not too cold."

Becoming a wine maker forced Ken to ask himself just what kind of wine he wanted to make.

"When I was twenty-two, I spent a year wandering around Europe," he says. "I fell in love with the bread, the cheeses, and the wines. I wanted to make wine—especially the reds—the way I remembered them tasting using oak barrels, without refrigeration or massive conditioning.

"In the countryside, you went to a small winery and filled up your own container from a large barrel. If you didn't have a cork they would give you an old corn cob. That's what I remember about wine: no sulfites, no filtration, no chemicals, no nothing. That's what I've tried to do with my Pinot Noir. That's what I drink. I take it right out of the fermentation tank.

Ken is the first to admit, however, that sulfites are necessary as they protect against outside bacteria and yeast contamination and stabilize the wine. But for his own, he'd rather not. Still, his Pinot Noir has caught on. "I started the Pinot for myself and now I sell a barrel a month. I'm surprised," Ken adds.

He makes two other red wines—Corrales Red, and a Red Table Wine—from a blend of Pinot Noir and Chancellor, with the blend adjusted to increase the fruitiness.

"The Corrales Red is more for people who don't like their reds dry, while the Red Table Wine is somewhere in the middle," says Ken.

Empty French oak barrels wait patiently in the courtyard of Las Nutrias Winery for the latest harvest.

Las Nutrias also produces six whites—Riesling, Chardonnay, Corrales White, a Blush and a Golden Blush, and Blanco Seco—with the idea of trying to make something to satisfy the broad spectrum of taste of his customers.

"I make wines from bone dry to very fruity," says Ken of his selection. "I do some Chardonnay in oak and some in stainless steel and they are two different wines. I cater to what my customers want, and they want a fruity (sweeter) wine. Half my sales are the blush wines.

"Remember," Ken adds, "many of my customers are going from Bud to a bottle of wine. But we are starting to get more demand for a dryer white."

Las Nutrias produces about 2,000 cases annually, depending on the grape harvest. Asked where he distributes, Ken admits that he does supply a couple of restaurants, but not from necessity. "Our wine is sold right out the front door. This year we will be sold out before Labor Day. No need to look further.

"We're a boutique winery on the verge of blossoming," Ken adds. "We have no intention of getting larger. We've been making these wines for four or five years with the same formulas and we sell everything we bottle."

He stops talking and looks about his winery with a satisfied eye, and then adds with a mischievous grin: "Mondavi doesn't have to worry about us, but we're having a great time with it."

WINES IN PRODUCTION

Pinot Noir; Proprietor's Red Table Wine (a blend of Pinot Noir and Chancellor grapes); **Corrales Red** (Chancellor grapes with some Pinot); **Riesling; Chardonnay; Corrales White** (Chardonnay grapes aged in stainless tanks); **Blush** (made from Chancellor grapes where the juice is taken off the skins immediately and allowed to ferment as a white wine); **Golden Blush** (from French hybrid Vidal Blanc grapes); and **Blanco Seco** (a blend of French hybrid Seyval Blanc and Riesling grapes).

Details: Las Nutrias Winery. Founded 1985. 4627 Corrales Road, Corrales, NM 87048. (505) 897-7863 or 898-5690. Tasting Room open Wednesday-Sunday from 12-6 pm, or by appointment. Proprietor and Wine maker: Kenneth Kendzierski.

THE TOUR CONTINUES

Upon leaving Las Nutrias, continue south for several miles past Alameda Blvd. to Paseo del Norte, turn left, cross the Rio Grande and turn right on Rio Grande Blvd. heading south. Continue south for about three miles to Anderson Valley Winery. About twenty acres of vineyards will appear on your left. The front entrance cannot be missed.

ANDERSON VALLEY VINEYARDS & WINERY

"My dad had a saying," recounts Kris Anderson, reminiscing about his late father, Maxie—the founder of Anderson Valley Vineyards in 1973 and the first hot air balloonist to successfully cross the Atlantic—"the road to success is strewn with the bodies of pioneers."

While that may well describe the early days of any business, it is certainly true for wine making in New Mexico. Since the late '70s, wineries have come and gone but Anderson Valley has managed to survive and grow into one of the major labels in the state producing about 18,000 cases per year.

"My father got into ballooning in the early '70s with the first world championships here in Albuquerque," says Kris, who now manages the winery in conjunction with his mother, Patty. "He was the CEO of a mining company. In the '60s and '70s, as he got around Europe on business, through France and Germany, he started ballooning and visiting local wineries.

"In 1973, dad put in a ten-acre trial vineyard by the house, but he put the rows too close. It was hard to get labor, and instead of buying the speciality European equipment used for narrow paced rows, he ended up plowing it all under. The next year, the vines he had plowed under came back up. So, we transplanted a few to a smaller plot and nursed them along."

A few years later, in 1981, the Andersons planted an additional nine acres, mostly French hybrids such as Baco Noir, Chancellor and Seyval, with some Cabernet and Merlot.

"Still, it was a hobby," Kris says. "My dad used to say he had to give the wine away because it was too expensive to sell."

When Maxie was killed in a balloon accident in 1983, the family decided to re-evaluate their hobby. By this time the vines Maxie had planted in 1981 were beginning to produce. So, in 1984, the family decided to apply for a commercial wine making license and go for broke.

"We bought some tanks and turned the balloon-making shed into the winery," remembers Kris. "It was the same shed where we built the Kitty Hawk—the balloon we used for the original trans-continental flight—and the Jules Verne, the one used for the unsuccessful around-the-world flight. Now, it is our bottling room."

King of Balloons

Until Maxie Anderson came along, no one had succeeded in crossing the Atlantic in a hot air balloon. Then in 1978, Anderson, along with his teammates, Ben Abruzzo and Larry Newman, flying the helium-filled balloon, Double Eagle II, dropped into an empty field on the outskirts of Paris completing their trans-Atlantic voyage.

Three years later, accompanied by his son Kris (now of Anderson Valley Winery) Maxie again did the impossible: the first trans-continental flight across North America in the

The winery's first commercial crush was in 1984, but marketing posed major problems. Kris and an employee loaded a van full of wine and made a mid-western swing to find distributors. The initial strategy was to try for areas where the California wineries were not strong.

"We went to Kansas City, Minneapolis, Milwaukee, St. Louis, Chicago and Indiana," remembers Kris. "Those were tough times. You have to have a reputation to reach out that far. The distributors liked our wines but they had to sell it to the consumer. Nobody knew New Mexico produced wine. Finally, we shrunk down to concentrate on New Mexico, Colorado, Arizona and Texas and our sales improve every year. We still sell in Chicago, though."

Anderson Valley wants to emphasize the production of premium and super-premium varietals. Most of the reds are in French oak although the intent is not a real oaky taste. The oak is for aging and taste, with some wines left to age for up to two years.

"We aren't making wines that we don't want someone to touch for years," says wine maker Phil Grossblatt, who joined the winery from Hallcrest Vineyards in the Santa Cruz Mountains of California, "but the Reserve Cabernet can be laid down for awhile. We are proudest of our Merlot, '92 vintage. Our new Merlot will be a bigger, fuller-bodied wine that will stay in the barrel longer. Everybody is waiting for it."

helium balloon, Kitty Hawk.

In June of 1983, Maxie was killed in a balloon accident in West Germany doing what he loved most, "climbing those mountains in the air." The Kitty Hawk now rests at the Smithsonian.

Asked about the difference in wine making in New Mexico as opposed to California, Grossblatt explains: "Its not much different except here the grapes are younger and wine makers are still trying to get used to the climate. While we don't have the varieties of grapes and sources that California wineries do, we are working with the same New Mexico grape growers and are developing greater control than before."

While Anderson Valley grows some grapes, they rely on vineyards farther south to supply most of the 120 tons crushed each year. Grossblatt makes several trips to the south each growing season to check on sugar levels and to discuss the optimum time to pick.

"We're more wine makers than grape growers," says Phil. "At some point we have to let them do what they do best and we do what we do best."

Although New Mexico has not yet attained the reputation of California and some of the other major grape growing regions, Kris Anderson is of the opinion that the viticultural areas of New Mexico rival those in any other part of the country.

"We've had some people say our Merlot is the best they've every tasted," says Kris. "We make a barrel-fermented Chardonnay. We've worked very hard on that particular wine—its one of the tougher ones.

We've done extremely well with our reds. When we talk about our best wines, we talk about our reds: Cabernet and Merlot."

One red Anderson uses for blending but does not sell is their New Mexico Ruby Cabernet.

"Our Ruby is probably better here than anywhere in the country," Kris claims. "It's an incredibly unknown variety for this region. It's one reason why our Cabernet and Merlot are so good. Hybrids here make some tremendous wine but they are unknown. We have to go with what sells."

Kris is proud Anderson Valley has turned the corner and is well on the way to becoming one of the strongest wineries in the Southwest.

"New Mexico has been through a weeding-out period," he adds. "We're one of the strong ones and we're still here. This business is very romantic, but I can tell you from years of hard work that any business is just business."

Anderson Valley was one of the pioneers of New Mexico wine, and to this day remains a leader.

WINES IN PRODUCTION

Chardonnay (made in the Montrachet-style in French Limousin oak barrels); **Sauvignon Blanc; Chenin Blanc; White Zinfandel; Balloon Blush** (a blend of Chenin Blanc, White Zinfandel and Ruby Cabernet); **Johannisberg Riesling; Claret; Merlot** (made from Merlot and Ruby Cabernet);

Cabernet Sauvignon; Private Reserve Cabernet Sauvignon (a wine rated 84 out of 100 by Wine Spectator magazine and the signature wine of Anderson; also, Gold Medal, 1994 Taster's Guild.

THE TOUR IS NEARLY OVER

At the completion of your visit with Anderson Valley Winery, your central wine tour is complete with the exception of Sabinal Vineyards south of Belen. If you choose not to continue to Sabinal, you may wish to end the day at one of Albuquerque's microbrew pubs: Assets Grille & Brewing Company, or the downtown Rio Bravo Restaurant and Brewery (food served at both).

The newest microbrewery, Rio Grande, is not a brewpub, but is open for tours. More information on Assets, Rio Bravo and Rio Grande can be found in the last chapter on microbreweries in New Mexico.

If you wish to visit Sabinal, turn left when exiting Anderson. Go south about one-quarter mile to Montaño, turn left and continue until you reach I-25. Take the Interstate south through Albuquerque towards Belen.

Enroute you will pass the Pueblo of Isleta, one of the largest, with a population of over 3,000. At the center of the Pueblo is a large mission church, built in 1629. Constructed at the north edge of the main plaza, it is said to be the burial site of Juan de Padilla, one of two Franciscan priests to have accompanied Coronado's expedition from Mexico in 1541. Juan stayed behind to convert the Indians. Occasionally, it is said, his body rises to perform miracles for the community.

Farther south is the town of Las Lunas named after the Luna family, who had established a large sheep ranch along the river in 1808. The Luna family exerted considerable influence over New Mexico politics during its territorial days (1849-1911).

Belen (original name possibly Bethlehem) remains a railroad town. In earlier years the town's merchants helped finance the Santa Fe Railroad to guarantee it would pass through their town, therefore ensuring further prosperity. Trains from Los Angeles to Chicago and from Denver to El Paso still converge at the large rail yards in the town.

South of Belen, leave the Interstate at exit #190 and continue south on Highway #116 through the town of Bosqué, about ten miles to Winery Road. Turn right and go under the Interstate through a narrow tunnel to Sabinal Vineyards, New Mexico's largest organic vineyard.

SABINAL VINEYARDS

What do you do when a winery fails? Make grape juice, of course, but make it pure and organic.

That's what happened to David and Ev Illsley of Sabinal Vineyards.

David, a gregarious man with a ready laugh, had retired from the Air Force and in 1981 a friend persuaded him to invest in a vineyard south of

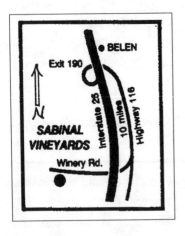

Albuquerque, near the town of Bosqué. The Illsleys did invest, focusing their efforts on ninety-five acres of vines and selling the grapes to a local winery.

When the winery failed five years later, David and Ev ended up buying the winery building. Now what? Tons of Vidal Blanc and Chancellor grapes were rotting on the vines for lack of a market. The answer was to harvest and bottle their own juice. Not just plain old grape juice, but fresh-squeezed, organically certified grape juice.

"Bottling pure grape juice was Ev's idea. I thought she was crazy," admits David. "But when I stopped laughing and started bottling, I knew she was onto something."

That was in 1989. Today, Sabinal, named after the old train stop just down the dirt road, is a certified organic vineyard and the only producer in the country of pure, organic grape juice. And the world is beating a path to their door.

"You have to have a niche for a product to sell, and my niche is pure organic juice," David says. "Every other juice in the grocery store is made from concentrate. I could do that too, but anybody could do it; just take concentrate and mix it with water.

"We're at the stage where our business is exploding. Demand is increasing tri-fold," David adds. "We're at 15,000 cases this year, and we're going to thirty. The reason is, this stuff is good! There's nothing like it in the marketplace. The white grape is one of the best natural sweeteners there is. The unadulterated juice tastes incredibly sweet yet contains not an ounce of processed sugar. There's no way in the world I can make enough to meet demand."

The Illsleys receive calls and letters from converts across the country who have tasted Sabinal's juice on trips to New Mexico and want to know where they can buy it. (Presently, the juices are distributed only in the Southwest and Northeast).

"New York is our biggest market because they want organic and can't get it," says David. "New York gourmet shops stock the juice and have asked us to produce a special 10-ounce bottle to satisfy their customers' demands."

Sabinal produces both red and white grape juices made from the vineyard's fruit. The grapes mature anywhere from mid-August to mid-October, meaning there is a six-week window in which to pick the grapes, stem and press them, and bottle the juice to supply the next year's inventory. Because the juice is pasteurized, it has an indefinite shelf-life. Sabinal also wholesales juice and grapes to winemakers in the state.

After the grape harvest and bottling, the Illsleys produce flavored apple juice—Apple Strawberry, Apple Red Raspberry, Apple Wild Cherry and Apple Cranberry—from Granny Smith and Golden Delicious apples grown in New Mexico, Arizona, Colorado and Washington. When the apples arrive from the orchard in large trucks, they are washed and pressed, the juice clarified, flavored, pasteurized and bottled.

So far, Sabinal's apple juices have not been certified organic. "I don't certify my apples as organic because I don't grow them," David says.

Beginning in 1994, however, Sabinal will begin to buy some certified organic apples and plans are in the works to certify his bottling plant as organic.

"This will be a wild, new adventure," David explains, "because there is no such thing as a certified organic plant in the state."

Sabinal Vineyards has endured all the frustrations and hardships of a small business since they hauled their first truckload of grapes to a bottler in Colorado in 1989, and then hauled the bottled juice back for resale because, in Ev's words, "we were so green."

People who know the product come back for more, and it it is largely word-of-mouth that has placed Sabinal where it is today.

As David says, "Once you taste our juice, you'll never drink anything else."

JUICES IN PRODUCTION

Sabinal produces two **organic grape juices**, a white and red, and three varieties of flavored natural apple juice: **Apple Strawberry; Apple Red Raspberry; Apple Wild Cherry;** and, **Apple Cranberry** in 10 oz. and 16 oz. bottles.

Don't Forget Bobby, Al and Al, Jr.

The Unsers, the most famous and successful racing family in the history of American auto racing, have been long-time residents of Albuquerque. Back in 1983, Al and his son, Al, Jr., became the first father-son racing team to compete against each other in the Indy 500. Al, Sr., who retired in 1994, is a four-time winner of the event as is his older brother, Bobby.

Al, Jr., gained notoriety in one Indy race by unsuccessfully trying to cut off a competitor's car to ensure his father's victory. Blood is thicker than water and around Albuquerque, the blood of the Unsers is thickest of all.

100

Visitors are welcome to the bottling plant where they may purchase organic grape and apple juices.

Details: Sabinal Vineyards. Founded 1989. 25 Winery Road, Bosqué, NM 87006. (505) 864-2816. Visitors welcome 11-5 daily. Tours by appointment. Proprietor and juice maker, David B. Illsley.

THE TOUR IS OVER

At the completion of your visit with Sabinal, you may return to Albuquerque by retracing your route on Interstate 25 north, or you may continue south toward Truth or Consequences and Elephant Butte Lake and the three wineries in that region. These wineries, however, are part of the southern tour to be covered in the next section.

The Southern Winery Tour

4

LA RVTA DE LAS VIÑAS DE LA REGIÓN DEL SVR

(The Winery Tour of the Southern Region)

INTRODUCTION

The tour of the eight southern wineries begins at the historic Old Mesilla (little hill) Plaza, and leads us through some of the most historic, rugged and arid regions of the Southwest, as well as the most fertile and visually stunning.

This tour also includes the lands where some of the first vineyards were planted by the Spanish over 350 years ago as well as modern New Mexico's largest and most productive pure vinifera vineyards.

While the first part of our tour, a day-long journey, will be limited to within a fifty-mile radius of Las Cruces, the largest city in southern New Mexico (pop 65,000) and the home of New Mexico State University, the second leg will take us on a sweeping, 350-mile, two-or-more day loop through the history book lands of southern New Mexico.

From Las Cruces, we will head northeast across the San Andres Mountains and through the White Sands National Monument to Alamogordo. From Alamogrodo, our route turns north bordering some of the famous Badlands of New Mexico *(El Malpaís)*, then curves back across the San Andres Mountains passing near the site of the first Atomic Bomb test to intersect the Rio Grande south of Soccoro.

At the Rio Grande and I-25, we will turn south paralleling the river in what the early Spanish explorers dreaded as the ninety mile, "Journey of Death" *(La Jornada del Muerto)*.

At Truth or Consequences, near Elephant Butte lake, the largest man-made body of water in the state, we will turn off for the three wineries near the town of Engle. Then, continuing south, our route will pass through the town of Hatch, the Chile Capital of the World, before returning us to Las Cruces.

THE FIRST DAY

On the first day, we will stay closer to home, visiting four wineries—La Viña, Blue Teal, Mademoiselle de Santa Fe, and St. Clair—each within an hour's drive.

Our tour begins at the historic Old Plaza in La Mesilla on the edge of Las Cruces. The Old Plaza, founded sometime around 1540, formed the core of early Spanish community life in the Mesilla Valley and was an important stop for Spanish soldiers, traders, Franciscan priests traveling *El Camino Real,* and later on, the Butterfield Overland Stage.

Mesilla itself took on increasing importance with time and by the 1850s, had became the most important town in the southwestern United States between San Antonio, Texas, and Los Angeles.

The Gadsden Purchase, which established the border between the United States and Mexico, was signed on the Old Plaza in 1854, and in 1858, the Butterfield Overland Mail and Stage Line established its regional headquarters at Mesilla. It was said the only place one could find a bed between San Antonio,

Texas, and California was at the Mesilla stage stop.

In 1861, a Confederate cavalry unit from Texas, intent on adding to the Confederacy, entered Mesilla and proclaimed the town the territorial capital of Arizona (in those days southern Arizona and southern New Mexico were one) for about a year until retreating back to Texas.

As a major center for social and business activities, Mesilla also attracted its share of crooks, gamblers and misfits. Billy the Kid and his cronies hung around the dance halls and bars of Mesilla in the 1870s, and it was at the courthouse-jail on the Plaza that The Kid was sentenced to be hung for murder. He escaped, however, before the sentence was carried out, killing two deputies in the process.

When the railroad bypassed Mesilla in favor of Las Cruces in 1881, the town went into decline. Soon after, the Doña Ana county seat was moved to Las Cruces spelling the end to three hundred years of commercial and social importance for the town and its plaza.

Cheap Seats

St. Louis to San Francisco for $150? It took 24 days of aches, bruises, gagging dust, lousy food, Indian attacks and not much sleep, but the Butterfield Stage Line was ready when you were.

In 1858, the stage line was started by John Butterfield to deliver mail for the U.S. Government. With 750 men, 1,800 horses, 300 yellow stagecoaches, and 200 way-stations every 12 miles along the 2,700 mile trail, it all cost $1 million.

Butterfield ran six coaches a week each way. Beginning at St. Louis, the route passed through Ft. Smith, AR., Ft. Worth and El Paso, TX., Mesilla, NM., Tucson, Los Angeles, Fresno, and San Jose, CA., before ending in San Francisco 3-1/2 weeks later. All for $150.

THE FIRST DAY TOUR BEGINS

Leaving the Old Plaza, turn right on Highway #28 going south. At University Ave, turn left heading toward the mountains and continue to Interstate-10. Once on the Interstate, head south toward El Paso and continue for about twenty miles, exiting at Anthony (#162).

Turn right onto State Road #404 and continue due west for about five miles. Soon State Road #404 will become O'Hara Rd. Continue straight through the housing district and across the railroad tracks. Turn right at Dairy Farm Road and drive across the Rio Grande. You are now on State Road #186.

Continue ahead until you come to a 'T.' Turn right on State Highway #28 going north. In less than one mile you will see the La Viña (the vineyard) sign on your right. Turn left down the dirt road to La Viña Winery, the oldest in the state.

LA VIÑA WINERY

"La Viña is the oldest continuously operated winery in New Mexico," says Ken Stark, a soft-spoken man with an open face that betrays just a hint of pride. "The original vines were planted in 1977, so we've got some pretty good root stock."

We were seated beneath a budding cottonwood in a small patio next to the winery. The warm sunshine was just beginning to coax life from

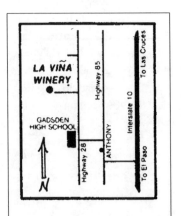

the seventeen acres of dormant grapevines that surrounded the main house.

The winery lies in the fertile La Mesilla Valley on the west side of the Rio Grande midway between El Paso and Las Cruces in an area where some of the first vines were planted by Franciscan priests 350 years ago.

"La Viña also hosts the oldest wine festival in the state, the original Wine Festival of New Mexico, begun back in 1982," Ken adds. "It's held the second weekend of every October. We invite about 5,000 of our closest friends," Ken chuckles, as he points toward an open area of grass behind the house. "Mostly from El Paso, where our label is well known. We have two stages for music, crafts, food, vendors, and we serve La Viña wine."

Ken and Denise Stark migrated from the panhandle of Texas to Albuquerque in the late '80s after a number of years ranching and farming. "We sold out and spent two months looking for a new home," Ken explains. "We thought California was the promised land until we got there. We finally settled on Albuquerque as the best medium-sized city in the Southwest."

Ken had taken wine appreciation courses while in Texas and found he had a pretty good sense of how wine should taste. "I owe my palate to the fact that I like food," says Ken, only partly in jest. "My wife and I love to eat and we're both pretty good cooks."

Shortly after arriving in Albuquerque, Anderson Valley Winery advertised for someone to help with the '89 crush. Ken volunteered and found himself a fast learner. "I picked up a pretty good understanding of the production of wine. After all, growing grapes is like agricultural production of any kind." Within a year Anderson asked Ken to take over production.

He stayed with Anderson until La Viña winery came on the market in 1992. The former owner worked with the Starks for a year, finally turning over the reins at the end of '93.

Ken found himself with a 1,500 case operation, with most of the wine being sold in grocery stores. The vineyard, planted in Riesling, French Colombard, Zinfandel, Ruby Cabernet, Cabernet Sauvignon, Chardonnay, and Sauvignon Blanc, also has a rare variety for New Mexico, the Carignane, and produces about sixty tons of grapes a year, enough for 10,000 gallons of juice.

Asked if he were happy with the mix of grapes, Ken sort of shrugs. "The whites are not particularly suited to this climate. It's too hot for most. The Rieslings don't work well here and the Sauvignon Blanc needs

An investment in French and American oak barrels is often necessary to age the best red wines.

to be picked young to get the varietal character out of it. The reds do well, though, especially the Italian reds."

Any new owner wants to leave his imprint on a business, and Ken Stark is no exception.

"Our goal is 5,000 cases of premium wine that we will sell only through restaurants. We don't want the La Viña label in the grocery stores. Historically, our label has been associated with premium wines, so we'll introduce a second label, Desert Flower, for our stainless fermented Chardonnay and Cabernet with a shorter time in the barrel. We'll sell these in the stores.

"Generally, we don't want to sell lower priced wines, so we've invested in seventy new French oak barrels. That's a lot of money. Our La Viña Chardonnay will be oak fermented. Our reds, too. Probably for eighteen months. With the economic pressures on a winery, very few can afford to age their wine that long. Even after eighteen months, our wines will need six months of bottle aging. We're taking a conservative, long term approach."

At the end of this process, the Starks plan on marketing only five varieties—Riesling, a white Zinfandel Blush, Cabernet Sauvignon, Zinfandel and Chardonnay. The Desert Flower line will have two varieties: Cabernet Sauvignon and Chardonnay.

Ken says that although many wineries are proud of bottling wine made only from estate grown grapes, he is more interested in achieving his style through blending. Of the 10,000 gallons of juice his vineyard produces, he will use only half and sell the rest. To make up the difference, he plans on buying juice from other vineyards in New Mexico and Texas.

"I don't feel I can get the complexity I want from just one vineyard," says Ken. "Many of the successful California wineries buy from all over the state, take the best, blend it together and make a good wine. That's what we plan to do.

"I saw a sign once in a store years ago: 'We mean to sell quality. We will sell it at a profit if we can, at a loss if we must, but we will sell quality.'"

That sums up how Ken Stark feels about La Viña.

WINES IN PRODUCTION

Under the La Viña label:

Zinfandel; Riesling (made from late harvest grapes and blended with Muscat); **Chardonnay** (Gold Medal, New Mexico State Fair); **Cabernet Sauvignon** (aged in oak 18 months. Should be laid down for a year); **Chamberino Blush** (made from a blend of white Zinfandel and Muscat Canelli).

Under the Desert Flower label:

Chardonnay (a milder, white table wine aged in stainless. Gold Medal, Southwest Wine Competition); and **Cabernet Sauvignon** (nine months in oak).

From the kitchen of Denise Stark:
Desert Flower Great Green Beans

Ingredients:

1 lb. fresh (or frozen) green beans	4 Tbs chopped green chile
4 Tbs butter	1/2 cup Desert Flower Chardonnay
1/2 medium onion, thinly sliced	2 Tbs piñon nuts
1 can beef or chicken broth	Freshly ground pepper to taste

Sauté the onion and chile in butter until soft. Add the green beans, broth and wine. Cook on high heat until almost all liquid is reduced. Add piñon nuts and serve along with a glass of La Viña Desert Flower Chardonnay.

🍷🍷🍷

Details: La Viña and Winery. Founded 1977. Box 440, Chamberino, NM 88027. (505) 882-7632. Vineyard and tasting room open in the summer, or by appointment. Proprietors/Wine makers: Ken and Denise Stark.

THE TOUR CONTINUES

Leaving La Viña, turn left on State Highway #28 and head north. We will be returning to the Mesilla Plaza via the old road that winds along beside the Rio Grande through some of the most fertile lands in New Mexico. You are also on the Don Juan de Oñate Trail, named for the Spanish explorer who colonized New Mexico for the Spanish Crown.

Increasingly, pecan orchards will appear on both sides of the road. Soon you will enter a three-mile stretch of mature pecans that tunnel the road. This is the Stahmann Pecan Farm, one of the largest in the world with 180,000 trees planted on 4,000 acres.

Founded in 1932, the farm now yields between 8 and 10 million pounds of pecans yearly without using insecticides. Ladybugs and other natural predators are used instead. Stahmann Farms is also the largest producers of pecans in Australia with a 2,000-acre farm in New South Wales. The Stahmann Country Store is on your left midway through the grove.

Continue north on Highway #28 direct to the Mesilla Plaza, where we began our tour earlier in the morning. Park on *Calle de Guadelupe,* which runs on the right (east) side of the Plaza, and walk down to the Blue Teal Winery tasting room, about one block south.

BLUE TEAL VINEYARDS

Hervé Lescombes, a handsome and generous man of French-Algerian descent, may well be the wine baron of southern New Mexico.

Starting with the Blue Teal label, which he founded in 1984, Hervé acquired the Mademoiselle de Santa Fe label in '89, and a year later took

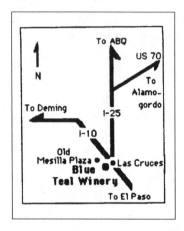

over the St. Clair label and winery outside of Deming, which at one time was the largest wine operation in New Mexico. The winery is now a production center for all three labels.

In addition to his other attributes, Hervé is foremost a survivor. "I was the first European (wine maker) in New Mexico in 1980, and I expect to be the last," he says quietly. In spite of water problems, root rot, marketing setbacks, and even a roof that recently caved in shutting down production at one facility, Lescombes' determination is evident.

Hervé was born in Algeria of French parents, but says, "In my heart, I do not consider myself French. I spent so much time in North Africa. Since 1885, my family grew olives and grapes in Algeria. I followed in my father's footsteps, producing a heavy red wine we sold to the French to blend to make their own wines better. It had lots of color, alcohol and tannin. Sometimes it was so heavy the French could make three liters from one.

"In 1962, at the end of the civil war, the Algerians pushed us out. We lost everything—our farm, winery, equipment and inventory. We returned to France where I farmed corn and wheat for a few years. Our farm was near Chablis.

"In 1970, there was a big increase in wine consumption and the government wanted to expand the boundaries of the appellation. I found I could plant 50 hectares (125 acres) in Burgundy grapes. We built a winery, Domaine de Perignon. Five years later we sold out."

Hervé planned to move to South America, but ended up in New Mexico when someone told him of investors who were looking for a wine maker. "I liked the country because it reminded me of North Africa," he says, referring to the wide open spaces and desert.

In 1981, Hervé planted the first commercial vineyards at Truth or Consequences. A year later he moved southeast to Lordsburg, planted 500 acres of viniferas and established the Blue Teal label. Then in '86 the root rot came, destroying many of the vines. The economy also changed at that time, from a weak to a strong dollar, and the European interests backing his ventures lost money overnight.

By '87, Hervé decided to regroup. He sold a winery operation he had in Texas, cut the national marketing of his Blue Teal label back to New Mexico, Arizona and El Paso, and decided to bypass distributors in favor of direct retail contact with the customer.

Lescombes, along with his two sons, Emmanuel and Florent, harvest 200-300 acres of vinifera grapes, and press up to 50,000 gallons yearly. Only 5,000-9,000 cases are bottled, however, about half of what they press. The balance of the juice is sold in bulk to California when the market is up.

When asked what makes a good wine, Hervé responds: "We have been in the wine business 100 years and I am still asking myself, what is a good wine? Danielle and I have a dry palate, but our best selling wines are always White Zinfandel and Muscat because they are sweet and southern New Mexico likes sweet wines. I never drink White Zin and Muscat. Our sparkling wine (Champagne) is dry for Las Cruces but sweet for us. He shrugs his shoulders, "So, who knows?"

Hervé admits the taste of his customers has gradually become more sophisticated. "We've trained a lot of people towards drier wines," adds his wife, Danielle. "They are changing. It's positive."

His philosophy? "First, make something California can't make. If you try to fight Gallo, no way. They can buy my wine in bulk, send it to California to bottle, send it back here and still beat me."

Hervé looks for specialty products he can retail direct to the customer from his tasting room, such as his 'Kirs'—sparkling wine flavored with raspberry liqueur, called Imperial Kir, and sparkling wine flavored with black currant, called Royal Kir. (The Kir process was started by a monk from Dijon, who gave it his name.) Both Kirs are offered in handpainted Champagne bottles.

To promote their wines, the Lescombes bought the old Fountain Theatre in Mesilla, just down from the Plaza, and turned the open patio into a tasting room where visitors can sample wines from both Blue Teal, and Mademoiselle (his second label), as well as the sparkling wine Kirs.

Danielle Lescombes, recognizable by her charming French accent, manages the tasting room. She often greets customers in French.

"The English language is difficult for her," smiles Hervé. "She tries to convince all Americans to speak French."

Danielle also runs the adjoining theatre, which shows classic and foreign films with subtitles. They draw a large audience from El Paso. Blue Teal wines by the glass and fresh popcorn can be enjoyed during the show.

"The problem with a winery," sighs Hervé, "is when you plant a new vineyard the first four or five harvests are not the best, but you can't lose the grapes. So, you have to begin your marketing using poor grapes at the beginning."

Hervé pauses, as if he's thinking over his past. "Waiting for grapes to grow, losing vines, waiting for your license. It's just a life."

WINES IN PRODUCTION

Hervé Lescombes bottles wine under three labels. Under the premium Blue Teal label:

White Cabernet (wine is fermented with the skins, then removed for a pink color); **Blanc de Blancs** (a blend of Thompson, Colombard, Chenin Blanc and Muscat); **Sauvignon Blanc**; **Chardon-nay**; **White Zinfandel**; **Riesling**; **Muscat**; **Zinfandel**; **Cabernet Sauvignon**; **Merlot**; and **Brut** (sparkling wine made from Chardonnay).

The Mademoiselle de Santa Fe and St. Clair wines are discussed below.

Details: Blue Teal Winery. Founded 1984. Calle de Guadelupe, Old Plaza, Mesilla, NM 88046. (505) 524-0390. FAX (505) 524-6962. Tasting Room hours: 1-5 daily. Proprietor/ Wine maker: Hervé Lescombes.

THE TOUR CONTINUES

Turn right from the Plaza to State Highway #28, and turn left heading north. Shortly, on the right, you will pass Meson de Mesilla, a thirteen room bed and breakfast with a first class restaurant. On your left, a short distance past the B & B is the Old West Brewpub, one of the New Mexico's newest microbrew pubs (for more information see the last chapter on microbreweries).

Continue north on State Highway #28, which changes to State Highway #292. Pass under Interstate-10 (the road changes to Motel Blvd.) and continue north until you intersect with U.S. Highway #70 (Picacho Ave). Turn left on #70 and cross the Rio Grande. Shortly beyond the river is a sign on your right for Mademoiselle de Santa Fe Winery.

MADEMOISELLE DE SANTA FE

Hervé Lescombes bought the Mademoiselle label in 1989 from a Swiss organization that had entered the American market a few years earlier. The intention of the Swiss was to capitalize on inexpensive land in New Mexico as an option to California. Miscalculations ranging from marketing problems, the changing world economy and the international overproduction of wine eventually forced the Swiss to sell.

Hervé, who had been hired by the Swiss to oversee operations, was a willing recipient. He leased the facility from the former owners and quickly expanded the operation by adding a kitchen, pit barbecue and an

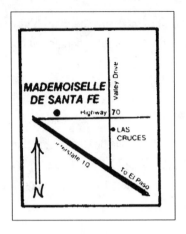

open air stage to host festivals and theatrical performances. It became a successful operation until the city decided an open theater was not allowed and a bout of bad weather caused part of the winery roof to collapse.

Undaunted, Lescombes continues to forge ahead. He is rebuilding the winery roof, enclosing the theater and expanding wine sales by the novel strategy (for New Mexico) of offering bulk sales of seven wines produced as organically as possible, (prices range from $1.85 to $2.35 a liter), in addition to bottle sales.

"We try to have natural wines here," says Hervé, "with a lower level of sulfites. Sometimes sulfites cause headaches. For your health, we have left out many of the chemicals in our bulk wine to make it as organically pure as possible."

Whether you bring your own bottle or buy one from the winery, directions are specific: If you supply your own, it may be any brand, any color glass, but 11-1/2 to 12 inches tall only, a 750 ml. bottle with a flat bottom. After you fill your bottle the winery provides a hand corking machine. Or you may buy an empty bottle for 35 cents, a cork for 15 cents, and reuse them on the next visit.

"Sometimes with our bulk organic wine, there is some sediment," concedes Hervé, "but we tell people, 'if you don't like the sediment, bring the wine back.' We also tell people to drink the wine within two or three days. Exposure to air changes the wine."

Hervé also notes that for wine kept in a refrigerator, crystallization may occur if it is kept very cold. This will not affect the wine.

Another service provided by Hervé is hand-painted wine bottles by a Las Cruces artist.

"It is a wonderful gift for birthdays, anniversaries or any occasion," comments Lescombes. "It is very reasonably priced." A customer interested in this service can fax in their own design.

"Our customers at Mademoiselle are very different from Blue Teal," adds Lescombes. "There is no competition. We sell a lot of bulk. It is very European. Everybody who drinks three or four bottles a week with their lunch or dinner, when they see our price, they do it."

WINES IN PRODUCTION, BULK OR BOTTLE

Chablis, **Chardonnay**, **Caber-net**, **Zinfandel**, **White Zinfandel**, **Muscat**, **Cabernet Sauvignon**, **Sauvignon Blanc**, **Riesling**, **Pinot Noir**, **Gewürztraminer**, and the following sparkling wines: **Brut**, **Royal Kir** and **Imperial Kir.**

Details: Mademoiselle de Santa Fe. Founded (as Binns Winery) in 1984. 3910 W. Picacho, Las Cruces, NM 88005. (505) 524-0481. FAX (505) 524-6962. Tasting room open daily 1-5 pm. Proprietor/Wine maker: Hervé Lescombes.

THE TOUR CONTINUES

The final winery on this leg of the tour is St. Clair, about 50 miles west, on the outskirts of Deming. To reach St. Clair, regain Highway #70 toward Deming. Within three miles, #70 melds with I-10. Continue west approximately thirty miles to the Akela exit (#102).

Take the overpass across the Interstate and turn right on the frontage road, which becomes State Highway #549. St. Clair Winery is fifteen miles down #549 on the right, just past Rock Hound State Park.

Towering stainless steel fermentation tanks are the hallmark of the European wine makers of southern New Mexico.

ST. CLAIR WINERY

At one time St. Clair winery was the largest operation in New Mexico and the Southwest. Like so many of the southern New Mexico wineries, St. Clair was started by European in-

terests in the early '80s with the idea of expanding their European operations into the United States.

The plant was designed and built on a grand California scale with a stemmer/crusher capable of processing 200 tons per day. The enormous bladder press is computer operated and the huge 30,000 sq. ft. building is lined with rows of gleaming 13,000 gallon stainless tanks.

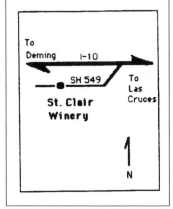

"Just one of these fermenting tanks," says Hervé, "is larger than most other single New Mexico wineries."

Hervé took over the St. Clair label in 1993, and it is in the giant tanks of the winery that Lescombes stores his bulk wine for shipment to California and other states, where it will be used for blending. The winery also processes all the wines for the Blue Teal and Mademoiselle labels, and as a special service, offers customized bottling under private labels.

There is a small tasting room and tours can be arranged for those passing through. St. Clair bottled wines are not generally available elsewhere but may be purchased on the spot.

WINES IN PRODUCTION

As this facility also processes wines for Hervé's other labels, vinifera wines available under the Blue Teal and Mademoiselle labels may also be purchased at the winery.

Wines include: **Muscat Canelli**; **White Zinfandel**; **Chardonnay**; **Sauvignon Blanc**; **La Clairette Red and White**; **Cabernet Sauvignon**;

and **White Cabernet.** Sparkling wines include: **Brut**, **Royal Kir** and **Imperial Kir** (also offered in hand painted bottles).

Details: St. Clair Winery. Founded 1982 by European interests. Label assumed by Hervé Lescombes in 1993. (505) 546-9324. Winery and tasting room located five mlles east of Deming on old Highway #549. Hours, 10-3 daily except Sunday. Proprietor/Wine maker: Hervé Lescombes.

THE TOUR RETURNS TO MESILLA

After your visit with St. Clair, retrace your steps on State Highway #549 to Interstate-10 going east. As you approach Las Cruces, exit at #140 to the Old Mesilla Plaza and the conclusion of the first day's tour.

You might be interested in visiting Las Cruces' other microbrew pub, O'Ryan's, located at Mesilla Valley Mall. Food is served. (See the last chapter on New Mexico microbreweries for more information.)

THE SECOND DAY TOUR BEGINS

Again, beginning at the Old Plaza in La Mesilla, head north on I-25 toward Albuquerque, then exit onto U.S. Highway #70 northeast toward Alamogordo, about seventy miles away.

As you climb into the San Andres Mountains, the road gradually rises to the 5,700-foot San Augustin Pass before descending the eastern side. Prior to the pass is the old mining camp of Organ, set against the spectacular Organ Mountains. In the 1870s, lead, copper and silver were mined in these mountains

On the eastern side of the pass, on your right, you will notice a displayed Army rocket signaling the beginning of the White Sands Missile Range, the famous Army testing range (open only for an annual tour in

October). Originally developed during the Second World War, the White Sands Proving Grounds (as it was then called) was used to develop and test new aircraft and rockets.

After the war, in 1948, the grounds were expanded (over much opposition by the local population) to include a great deal of surrounding land, including much of the Tularosa Valley, the Organ and Hueco Mountains and the entire San Andres range. Occasionally, Highway #70 is closed for a short time for missile firings. A sign along the road (with blinking lights) will inform you if the road is closed.

Continue on for thirty miles to the White Sands National Monument. Dedicated by Congress in 1934, the Monument consists of 224 square miles of pure surface gypsum (hydrated sulfate of calcium), one of only three such surface deposits of pure gypsum in the world. There are picnic and camping facilities at the Monument headquarters and plenty of wide open spaces for digging your barefeet into the mountains of white sand.

Fifteen miles beyond White Sands is the town of Alamogordo (Spanish for 'fat cottonwood'), the home of Holloman Air Force Base, established during WWII to test new aircraft, and the International Space Hall of Fame. Constructed in 1976, the Space Hall

I'd Like A Room, Please

Gus Hilton, in the 1880s, was known as the 'Merchant King of San Antonio, (NM).' He ran the largest general store between Albuquerque and El Paso and started a stagecoach line that crossed the mountains to White Oaks, just north of Carrizozo, to service the mining industry.

Gus's son, Conrad, was born on Christmas Day in 1887. A few years later, Conrad, noting the absence of hotels in his little town, rented rooms in the family home. Bedding was guaranteed to be changed at least once a week no matter how many had slept between the sheets.

Today, Conrad's first Hilton Hotel in San Antonio has become a chain of 400 hotels that span the world.

features displays and information on equipment used in space exploration.

From Alamogordo, continue northward on U.S. Highway #54 toward the town of Tularosa. Four miles north of Alamogordo is Eagle Ranch, the state's first and largest pistachio nut farm, with 85 acres and 13,000 trees. Tours are available year around from the gift shop located on the highway.

Tularosa, named after the reeds that inhabited the nearby river (*Tular* meaning, 'a reedy place'), is also known as the 'City of Roses.' Each May the city holds its annual Rose Festival.

Approximately two miles north of town is the Tularosa Vineyards and Winery.

TVLAROSA VINEYARDS

"If a Cabernet doesn't tear your throat out it isn't any good," quips Dave Wickham, owner and winemaker of Tularosa Winery. "Wise people do well to lay a Cab down, but I like wine like that. I like a fresh Cabernet, I really do."

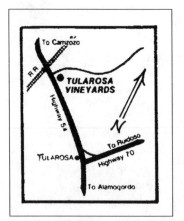

Dave recognizes, however, that most people don't share his taste for a fresh Cabernet or Merlot, so he leaves them in the barrel a little longer than he would for himself. And the effort has paid off. His '90 and '91 Cabs and '92 Merlot have won medals at the Southwest Wine Competition and are the signature wines of Tularosa.

"I didn't start out in this business as a professional," Dave continues, "so I have this idea that wine ought to be as natural as possible. Just go out, pick the grapes, bring them in, jump on them and put them in a barrel. You should be able to reach into the barrel a few months later and pull out some good wine. If you're not making good wine naturally, you're doing something very wrong."

Wickham grew up on a farm near Watkins Glen in the Finger Lakes region of New York. His family were early settlers of the region and had a winery at one time, so his love of grapes stems from childhood memories. A career in the Air Force brought him to New Mexico.

When he retired in the '80s, Dave wanted to get back into farming. He planted a few grapevines in Tularosa as a hobby and found they did well. So, he began talking to experts, read every wine making and grape-growing book he could find and consulted with the agricultural people at New Mexico State.

In 1985, convinced that a vineyard on the eastern side of the San Andreas mountains was feasible, Wickham bought ten brush-covered acres north of Tularosa and turned an abandoned military building into his winery.

Five acres are currently planted in viniferas—Grenache, Merlot, Chenin Blanc, Sauvignon Blanc, Zinfandel, Muscat Canelli, Chardonnay, Brunello and Nebbiollo. The last two are Italian varieties he planted for experimental purposes.

"I think I'm the only grower of Grenache in the state," says Dave. "I also think I'm the only winery that uses Muscat Canelli as a pure vinifera and not as a blend." The Brunello (also known as Sangiovese Grosso) is a rare grape. "I saw Lee Iacocca holding a bottle of Brunello on the cover of *Wine Enthusiast* magazine," Dave adds. "I've been told if you can produce a high quality wine, you can get up to $50 a bottle in the right market."

But then Dave admits it may not work out. "With the Italian varieties, if we can't make at least a barrel of wine, it's outta here. We'll use them as blenders to add complexity to our other wines."

While Dave planted his first vines in 1985, he didn't bottle until '89, and then only three varieties—Chenin Blanc, Cabernet Sauvignon and Grenache. Since then the winery has increased production to about a thousand cases a year of about eight different wines, all vinifera.

Included in the eight varieties are two novelty wines, a Sangria to fulfill local demand for a sweet wine, or as Dave phrases it, "for your aunt who doesn't normally drink wine," and the Mission, his tribute to the early Spanish colonial days of New Mexico.

The basis for Wickham's Sangria is Chenin Blanc that is fermented along with grape skins left over from the Zinfandel, Cabernet and Merlot to give the wine its red color. He adds grape juice for sweetness and orange and lemon juice for flavoring.

"It's a hot day drink," says Dave. "Pour it over ice cubes and its like drinking lemonade. But watch out. It'll sneak up on you."

The Mission wine is another story. No one in New Mexico is growing Mission grapes commercially so Dave has had to buy his grapes from private backyards.

"It's been a great seller, when we can get the grapes," says Dave. "The supply wasn't large enough or dependable enough for us to continue, so we planted our own Missions. It's not only historically correct for New Mexico, its something different. Small wineries need to be different."

Dave prefers to produce all his wine from estate grown grapes and not buy grapes from other vineyards. So far, that has not been possible. He produces only enough for half his needs, so Wickham has recently planted another 2,000 vines.

"You have to be careful what you plant. My advice to small vineyards and wineries is to stay away from heavy producing grapes because you can always buy them on the market cheaper than you can grow them. They produce a lot of wine, but that's not what you want. You want quality.

"If we have to buy more than 50% of our grapes for blending, our Cabs and Merlot don't do as well. That tells me something about our location. My grapes grow under hardship. That old saying about grapes grown under hardship seem to make better wine comes through here."

Most of Wickham's production is sold from his tasting room with the rest marketed through grocery stores in Alamogordo. "Wine sales are tough," admits Dave.

"Remember, my clients are Coors drinkers. We're cowboys and Indians down here," he laughs. "That's the way it works."

WINES IN PRODUCTION

Chardonnay; Chenin Blanc (Dave's back porch, 'hamburger' wine); **Muscat Canelli; Blush; Zinfandel; Merlot** ('Highly Recommended' by Southwest *Internacional* Wine & Food Review); **Cabernet Sauvignon** (Silver Medals at the Southwest Wine Competition for '90 and '91 vintages);

Grenache; Mission (an historic wine of distinctive earthy taste and aroma. Produced when grapes are available); and **Sangria** (Tularosa's novelty wine made with Chenin Blanc and added orange, lemon and grape juices for flavor and sweetness).

Details: Tularosa Vineyards. Founded 1985. Star Route 2, Box 5011, Tularosa, NM 88352. Located two miles north of Tularosa on Highway #54. Phone (505) 585-2260 or 585-4414. Winery open daily year round from 12-5. Proprietor/Wine maker: Dave Wickham.

Dave Wickham offers his favorite 'down-home' recipe for Red Bean/ Red Wine Skillet.

Ingredients:

3 Tbs olive oil	1 medium yellow onion, chopped
1-3 garlic cloves, chopped	1/2 pound picnic ham, cut into
1 tsp dried thyme	1/2-inch cubes
2 cans red kidney beans, drained	1 tsp Tabasco sauce
1 cup Tularosa red Zinfandel	

Pour olive oil into a heavy skillet. Sauté garlic and onion. Add remaining ingredients, cover and simmer over medium heat for 25-30 minutes. Serve with French bread, tossed salad and a glass of Tularosa Zinfandel while cooking and when eating.

THE TOUR CONTINUES

Continue north on Highway #54 through the town of Three Rivers, originally the rail station for the Three Rivers Ranch, which shipped its cattle to eastern markets from this location in the 1870s on the Southern Pacific Railroad. According to legend, the Ranch also assisted Billy the Kid in shipping his rustled cattle to market, for a small cut, of course.

At the town of Oscuro, you have entered Lincoln County, in its early days the largest county in the United States, and after the Civil War, one of the most bloody places in the country.

The Lincoln County War was the result of friction between two contrary cultures—the agrarian and Catholic old-time Spanish settlers and the newly arrived English and Protestant cattlemen from Texas and beyond. The resentment smoldered for years, finally erupting in a three-year war (1878-81), which claimed its share of lives.

While not the bloodiest range war on record, this one attracted Billy the Kid, who grew up in Hondo, about fifty miles to the east. He roamed the New Mexico Territory from Ft. Sumner in the east to Silver City in the west, developing quite a reputation along the way.

Upon leaving Oscuro, look to the Northwest, toward part of the famous 'Badlands of New Mexico' *(El Malpaís)* and the Oscuro Mountains beyond. What is not visible is the

Never Kid A Kid

In 1876, when William Bonney killed his first man at age 16, his mother said: "My son's such a kidder!" The name stuck and Willie became known as 'Billy the Kidder.'

A while later, when Billy shot a Sheriff in the Lincoln County War, people said Billy wasn't 'kidding around anymore.' Out of respect, his name was

mushroom cloud that hung over these mountains for a few earth-shaking minutes some fifty years ago.

Only forty-five miles away, behind the Oscuro Mountains, is Trinity Site, where the first Atomic Bomb was exploded on 16 July 1945, an event that changed all of civilization.

The tour bears left onto U.S. Highway #380 at the town of Carrizozo, named after the carrizozo grass that is native to the land and has historically provided great livestock feed.

Carrizozo, like so many small towns in the West, owed its founding and existence to the railroad and paid the price of railroad modernization when the new longer range diesel locomotives of the Southern Pacific soon made small maintenance towns obsolete.

Leaving Carrizozo traveling west on U.S. Highway #380, you are beginning the sixty-six mile drive across the San Andres Mountains into the

shortened to 'Billy the Kid.'

When his mother was told, on Billy's 21st birthday, he had killed 21 men, she said: "You've got to be kidding!"

When Sheriff Pat Garrett hauled Billy to La Mesilla to be hung, the Kid made a daring escape killing two deputies. When told of the breakout, his mother said, "I told you. Never kid a kid."

A year later, Garrett shot Billy at Ft. Sumner ending the life of the greatest kidder of all time. This is the mostly true story of Billy the Kid. No kidding!

Rio Grande Valley on the other side. A few miles out of town the road crosses a sea of black volcanic rock, believed to be the remains of the most recent lava flow—about two thousand years ago—in the continental United States.

The Valley of Fires State Park, on your left, is a prime example of *El Malpaís,* the famous badlands, where the land is so inhospitable (from volcanic activity) it is virtually impossible to cross, making it a favorite hiding place for many of early New Mexico's most famous banditos.

Modern day hikers will wear out a pair of boots from one day of struggling over the volcanic debris of *Malpaís.*

The town of Bingham is another of those small towns that flowered for a brief spell to provide support for local mining operations. Only a few old buildings remain. Twenty-five miles beyond, you will cross the Rio Grande and enter the town of San Antonio, another mining town that prospered during the coal boom of the 1880s.

Just prior to San Antonio, turn left on State Road #1, across from the Owl Bar and Cafe, famous for its Green Chili Cheeseburgers, and head south paralleling Interstate 25 for *Bosqué del Apache* (woods of the Apache) National Wildlife Refuge.

Established by the U.S. Fish and Wildlife Service in 1939, *El Bosqué* is a fifty-seven thousand acre thicket of old cottonwoods, willows and creeping tamarisk that relies on the unpredictable waters of the Rio Grande for sustenance.

The river binds the plant life to the unforgiving soil and offers thousands of ducks, cranes and geese a refuge on their annual migration south, as well as a safe haven to hundreds of other species of mammals and reptiles.

While the best bird viewing is during early morning or late evening between October and February, wildlife inhabit *El Bosqué* year-round and offer a glimpse both of history and nature, if even from your car window.

Highway #1 joins Interstate-25 about eight miles south of the wildlife refuge. Regain I-25 south toward Truth or Consequences, a distance of about forty-five miles, to visit the next wineries on our tour—Chateau Sassenage, Domaine Cheurlin and Duvallay.

While riding in the comfort of your car, you may still look eastward across the river to the base of the San Andres Mountains and the route of the Journey of Death *(La Jornada del Muerto).*

The Journey was actually a ninety-mile shortcut taken by early Spanish explorers and settlers trying to knock days off their travel between Las Cruces and Socorro. It was a grueling eight-to-ten day march (often at night to avoid the heat) devoid of water and food, and open to attack by the fierce Apache, who had adopted the horse from the Spanish and now used it effectively in hit-and-run raids against the very people who had imported the animal into New Mexico.

While still several miles from Truth or Consequences, you will be able to see fingers of Elephant Butte Lake, the largest man-made body of water in New Mexico, created by damning the Rio Grande to provide flood control, irrigation and electricity. The lake is fifteen miles long with over 220 miles of sandy beach shore. Camping and picnicking facilities are provided at the state park on the lake.

To visit the three wineries located east of the lake, take the first exit off the Interstate for Truth or Consequences and drive into the center of town.

At the first (and only) stop light, turn left on State Road #51, and leave town on the fifteen-mile excursion to Engle. The narrow road winds its way past the Elephant Butte Dam and up onto the higher plateau in back of the lake.

At this point, the vast expanse of arid, high mountain desert that seems to roll on forever provides a glimpse of what it must have been like to have struggled through the Journey of Death three hundred years ago.

What's In A Name?

In 1950, Ralph Edwards, host of one of the most popular radio programs of all time, 'Truth or Consequences,' issued a national plea upon the show's tenth anniversary:

"I wish some town in the United States liked our show so much it would change its name to Truth or Consequences."

The people of Hot Springs, New Mexico, tired of being just another town, responded with enthusiasm. Truth or Consequences immediately put the town's few hundred residents on the national map, but created writer's cramp in the process.

Today, people in the know refer to the town simply as, 'T or C.'

Two or three miles short of Engle, a large vineyard will appear on your right. Immediately to your left is a dirt road that passes through two low brick columns. Turn left down this road and continue for about three miles to a substantial metal building surrounded by hundreds of acres of grape vines.

You are now in the Armendariz Valley and the largest concentration of grapes in New Mexico. This is also the winery for Domaine Cheurlin and Duvallay, two separate labels with their own vineyards but sharing the same processing plant.

DOMAINE CHEURLIN

Patrice Cheurlin, short and stocky with a black beard and a quick, erupting laugh, seems out of place in the solitary, metal building that is the Domaine Cheurlin winery amidst the expanse of chamisa, juniper and cactus at the base of the San Andres Mountains.

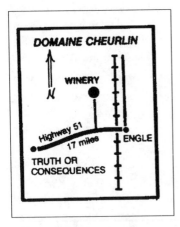

From one dusty window it is possible to gaze across acres of grapevines to the waterless, forboding land on the horizon known to the early Spanish as the 'Journey of Death,' and wonder how this young, easygoing Frenchman came to the vastness of the American Southwest.

To the self-proclaimed playboy who grew up in the Champagne region of France, taught SCUBA diving for the French Army on the beaches of Tahiti and flew his own plane (and continues to do so between his home in Albuquerque and the vineyards east of T or C), coming to New Mexico with his father in 1983 was a shock.

"I had a very good life in France—a nice house with a garden and a sports car," Patrice recalls, somewhat wistfully. "My father makes Champagne (*Champagne de Richelun*) in Épernay. My mother comes from a winemaking family in Burgundy. So, when I came here with my father, it was very difficult.

"My father wanted to invest in the United States. He bought some land to start a research center for grapes. We experimented with seven or eight varieties on 75 acres, only vinifera—Merlot, Cabernet, Chardonnay, Riesling—to see what would survive the winter. What survived best were the Chenin Blanc, Chardonnay, Pinot Blanc and Pinot Noir. When my father found we could make some good wine, we built a winery in 1985 and started to make sparkling wine, *Méthode Champenoise.*"

Since then, Cheurlin has focused only on two sparkling wines, a Brut and an Extra Dry, although he is about to introduce an estate grown Cabernet Sauvignon and a Chardonnay.

Patrice worked under his father's direction for three years. When his father finally turned the business over to his son, Patrice decided he needed to make some changes.

"My father tried to make Champagne the European style—very dry. But it is difficult to sell that style in the Southwest. You have to satisfy the demands of your market, so I began to make something a little bit fruitier (sweeter) in the American style."

But not everything is American. Patrice still make his sparkling wine the French way, with French techniques, including riddling, or turning all the inverted bottles in the wood racks by hand. It's the finishing that has changed. Patrice adds more *'liqueur'* (wine and sugar) to the last stage to achieve a fruitier taste.

Of the 2,500 cases of sparkling wine produced each year, two-thirds are marketed in New Mexico and Colorado. The other third, about 700 cases, is exported to Taiwan, Hong Kong and Japan. Exporting is expensive, Patrice admits, but he doesn't have to pay the domestic Champagne tax of $3.40 per gallon on what is exported. That makes it more profitable, so Patrice is pushing the export market.

Cracking the Far East market is more than a problem of shipping. "They don't know much about wine," Patrice adds. "We have to give a lot of seminars on wine. We have to do a lot of promotion. Wine is not really part of their life."

The promotion and seminars are paying off. Cheurlin has recently signed a contract with a Japanese restaurant chain that will quadruple exports to that country, forcing an increase in his own production. Asked if he will have the grapes, Patrice replies that he only has 75 acres of vines, but if necessary, he could expand into the other 800 acres the family owns.

How would Cheurlin like to see Americans drink Champagne? "Like they do in France," he responds with a laugh. "Everyday, with every meal." Then he stops laughing and turns serious.

"In France the market is changing a lot. They are buying a lot of good sparkling wine from Spain. It is cheaper. The price difference is forcing French Champagne makers to change their production (looking for faster methods rather than letting the Champagne age naturally in its bottle for years). It is becoming more like America because of the price. The French will buy two bottles of Champagne for special occasions, but ten bottles of sparkling wine, maybe from Spain."

As to the wine industry in New Mexico, Patrice thinks it will be another ten years before New Mexico wine will be recognized.

"People still don't know New Mexico wine," he laments. "They think we make bad wine, that we can't do something nice. But we can produce good wine, as good as California. It is not the wines, but the marketing, the perception. That will take time."

Asked if he will be around to see New Mexico wine mature, Patrice smiles: "I don't miss France anymore. I think 100% American."

WINES IN PRODUCTION

Domaine Cheurlin specializes in two sparkling wines, *Méthode*

Champenoise, and will soon market a **Chardonnay** and a **Cabernet Sauvignon**.

Brut (made from a 90:10 blend of Chardonnay and Pinot Noir grapes. A consistent Gold Medal winner at the New Mexico State Fair); and **Extra Dry** (an 80:20 blend of Chardonnay and Pinot Noir estate grown grapes).

Details: Domaine Cheurlin. Founded 1984. Office: 500 Main St, Truth or Consequences, NM 87901. (505) 894-0837. Winery 15 miles east of town. (505) 894-3226. Winery open weekdays from 7-3:30 p.m. Call for an appointment on Sat & Sun. Proprietor/wine maker: Patrice Cheurlin

DUVALLAY VINEYARDS

"We were the first to plant vineyards around here and the last ones to put wine in the bottle. We are very slow," says Fernando Gonzalez, general manager and winemaker for Duvallay Vineyards. "Our idea was to come to the market with something very special. The grapes were planted in 1982. The first year we bottled was 1990."

A tall, trim and very charming Spaniard fluent in four languages, Fernando tips his Panama hat as he comes in from the dusty fields revealing a well-trimmed mustache and dark eyes set in a handsome face. He selects a bottle of his favorite Duvallay wine, Pinot Blanc, and fills three tulip-shaped glasses as we settle in for a chat.

A native of Spain, Fernando grew up in the northeastern wine region where his grandfather's family owned vineyards for many centuries. "I hated visiting my grandfather's vineyard when I was young," Fernando confesses, "because there was always work to do. I much preferred

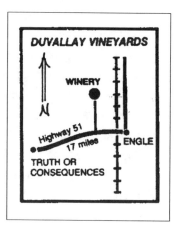

visiting my maternal grandmother's farm. She had horses and cows. I loved to ride the horses and always dreamed of having a ranch some-day," he says.

When Fernando left home in 1972 to study law in Switzerland, he was obliged to pay his own way since his father refused if his son would not study in Spain. In search of extra income, Fernando began working for Paul Girardet, a well-known Swiss wine maker.

"Girardet taught me to enjoy working in the vineyard and to love wine," says Gonzalez, raising his glass of Pinot Blanc for a toast. "How do you like this wine?" he asks. "Pinot Blanc is our most popular wine. It is the only one in New Mexico. There is very little of this wine in the United States." The Pinot Blanc is a balanced wine with a delicate taste that has won in blind tastings against its Swiss counterparts.

Fernando refills his small glass carefully, as if he is pouring a vintage Champagne.

"Girardet convinced me to switch from the study of law to viticulture and Oenology," Gonzalez continues. "I worked for Girardet in the vine-yard, winery and nursery for ten years. I learned to make wine the Swiss way, dry and light. After that, I needed a change, so I traveled a lot, to Argentina and Mexico, to many countries."

Returning to Geneva, Fernando began working for Jean Zanchi, the largest wine importer and distributor in Switzerland. Zanchi had recently bought an interest in a vineyard near Truth or Consequences and in 1986, he asked Gonzalez to oversee the new operation.

"When I agreed to come, I thought it would only be for a few months," Fernando says, with a wry smile. "But here I am. Everything I learned about wine making before coming here is not useful in New Mexico. Everything here is so different. The plants need to be cared for in a different way and the wine is different, too."

The Duvallay vineyards have had their problems. When the Euro-pean interests began buying land around T or C in the early '80s, every-one in Europe had money. Sometime after 1985, however, the economy changed all over the world and many of the European operations in New Mexico went out of business.

Fernando Gonzalez, wine maker for Duvallay Vineyards, extolls the virtues of his Swiss-style Pinot Blanc.

As for Duvallay, "We suffered here," laments Gonzalez. "With a winery, you always have to look twenty years down the road. So we started slowing down on the operation. We didn't have very good harvests. There were lots of problems with the frost in '87 that killed many plants. We had to start over."

Today, Fernando oversees 150 acres of vinifera wines and produces around 7,000 cases of six wines, all from estate-grown grapes—Pinot Noir, Cabernet, Riesling, Chardonnay, Pinot Blanc and Sauvignon Blanc. Production is limited to one ton of grapes per acre with a yearly yield of 100-150 tons, depending on conditions.

Fernando's wines are light and delicate, very much like those produced by his Swiss mentor, Girardet. "I try to make the wine the way I learned in Switzerland—dry, with low sugar and alcohol," says Gonzalez.

The wines also reflect his personal style. "I personally don't like to touch the wine too much; you have to let the wine do its work. I filter one time before putting the juice in the tanks and then I filter once again before bottling."

Gonzalez ferments in stainless steel tanks, then ages the wine briefly in wood. He does not like too much oak in the wine, especially the whites.

"I remember tasting California wine fifteen years ago and it tasted like they mashed a piece of wood in it. They are getting better. California wines have a smoother taste now.

"Personally," Fernando adds, "I like some wood with red wine—the strong wines like Cabernet or Pinot Noir, but I do not like to put white wines in wood."

In between harvests and wine making, Gonzalez still indulges his passion for travel. Every few months the bachelor is off to Geneva, Argentina or his home in Spain. Yet, he always returns to T or C to tend to the vineyards and the delicate aging of the wines.

WINES IN PRODUCTION

All wines are made in a light, Swiss-style from 100% estate-grown grapes.

Pinot Blanc (The signature wine of Duvallay, it is most comparable to a Swiss wine and has been favorably rated in blind tastings in Switzerland); **Chardonnay; Riesling**; **Pinot Noir**; and **Cabernet Sauvignon.**

Details: Duvallay Vineyards. Founded 1982. Office, 500 Main St, Truth or Consequences, NM 87901. (505) 894-7122. Winery fifteen miles to the east on Highway #51. Open daily except weekends, 7 a.m. to 3:30 p.m. (505) 894-3226. Call for appointment Sat & Sun. Owner: Jean Zanchi & Son (of Switzerland). Manager/wine maker: Fernando Gonzalez.

THE TOUR CONTINUES

The third winery, Chateau Sassenage, is generally not open to visitors, although a phone call in advance to the manager and wine maker, Jean-Marie Guillaume, would probably solicit an invitation. You can, however, taste the wines produced by Chateau Sassenage at the winery's office in T or C, with a phone call in advance.

The Sassenage office is adjacent to Jean-Marie's home, located two blocks off Highway #51, as you are entering town on your return from Engle. If Jean-Marie is in the vineyards, his wife Sabine will welcome you.

CHATEAU SASSENAGE

No two towns could be more visually and culturally opposite than Truth or Consequences, New Mexico, and Verzenay Champagne, France. So one can imagine the surprise of young Jean-Marie Guillaume, wine maker and manager of New Mexico's largest vineyard, when he first arrived in the Land of Enchantment on his honeymoon a decade ago.

A fifth-generation member of a Champagne-producing family, he grew up working in the small, lush region of Champagne. His wife, Sabine, also comes from a family in Champagne. Yet, he was looking for a change and, intrigued by the challenge of planting vines in the virgin lands of the

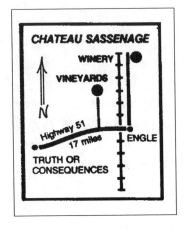

Southwest, accepted an offer from his family investment company to plant a vineyard in the vast, open plains of New Mexico in 1983.

"We came here on our honeymoon," says Jean-Marie. "I guess we are still on our honeymoon because we never left."

After his initial success, two other European investment groups asked him to manage their vineyards as well. Jean-Marie organized the three into a co-op with three labels—Chateau Sassenage, Sabine and Mont-Jallon—all working under the same license with Jean-Marie as the wine maker.

Dressed in blue jeans and khaki shirt, a golden retriever at his heels, the tall and elegant Jean-Marie greeted us with his French accent in the front yard of his unpretentious T or C home and led us into his office where he offers tastings to interested buyers.

A couple from California had just left with a case of his Chateau Sassenage Cabernet Sauvignon; they had tried a bottle at a restaurant in Albuquerque and couldn't wait to share their find with friends back home in San Francisco.

With the birds singing and warm sun streaming in the open door on a balmy February afternoon, Jean Marie's warm blue eyes smile when asked what he tells his friends back in France about living in T or C.

Jean-Marie holds up his hand. "First, we must have some wine," he interrupts, "otherwise, how can we speak about it?. Let the wine enhance what we have to say."

He expertly fills three flutes from a bottle of Mont-Jallon sparkling wine. The bubbles rush to the top under a layer of white foam that hesitates precisely upon reaching the rim. Then he answers the question with a smile: "Three-hundred-twenty days of sunshine. That's what I tell my friends.

"I grew up working in the vineyard and winery of my family in Champagne," he continues. "It has been a big change to come here. We came from the green land, with a little tiny piece of land for a vineyard, down to a half or a third of an acre, and the vines are planted 3 feet by 3 feet by 3 feet high. You are always bent on your knees to work in the vineyard over there. But you come here, you have thousands of acres, no more trees, the sun all the time, and you can work by standing up; that is a big advantage."

Before coming to New Mexico, he worked six months in a California winery to learn English and get a feel for the American market. It was long enough for him to discover the three big wine grapes in America—Cabernet, Chardonnay and Pinot Noir.

"Coming from Champagne, I knew Chardonnay and Pinot Noir; those are the two kinds of grapes we grow over there," says Jean-Marie. "So, in T or C, we didn't mess with anything else than Chardonnay and Pinot Noir in our first vineyards."

Of those eighty acres, known as the Engle Vineyard, sixty acres are planted in Chardonnay and twenty in Pinot Noir. Both have done very well, although the Pinot Noir takes twice as long to establish. Four years ago he added Cabernet, Merlot and Zinfandel.

The second vineyard he was asked to manage was already planted with Riesling and Chenin Blanc. Those grapes are a tough sell, according to Jean-Marie, because the wines are not as popular, although the grapes make very good wine.

The third vineyard is planted in Cabernet Sauvignon, Sauvignon Blanc, and Merlot. The three operations total 280 acres of vines, making this European Co-op the largest vineyard in New Mexico and a supplier to many of the state's other wineries.

Jean-Marie produces about 5,000 cases from his estate-grown grapes for the three labels, each having a distinct style, and all distributed in New Mexico. Mont-Jallon, named after a family vineyard in Champagne, offers a Brut and a Blanc de Noirs. Sabine, named for his wife, produces five wines including a lighter-style, fruity Cabernet Sauvignon. Both labels came on the market in '93.

Chateau Sassenage has been on the market since 1990 with its trademark big Cabernet. With more tannin and complexity than his other Cabernet under the Sabine label, the Sassenage Cab, ideally, should be aged for three years after its release to be at its peak. Since most American consumers do not lay wine down to age, Jean-Marie is aging the wine an extra six months before releasing it.

He is hoping the Sassenage Chardonnay will become a trademark as well. Realizing that a French-style Chardonnay—crisp and dry—does not fare very well in competitions, he now ages in French oak but still aims for a crisp, balanced wine. Being French, he believes wine should pair with food, not mask it.

"Wine is not supposed to cover the food, wine is supposed to go with the food. But you still have to taste the food over the wine. Not the opposite."

When asked about the French Paradox (the recent study that reports a relative absence of heart disease among the French due, in part, to red wine), Jean-Marie replies:

"We drink more wine, but less Coke, Pepsi and all those soft drinks, and we don't drink hard liquor. Yes, we have cream sauce, cognac sauce with steak, or Champagne sauce with fish. We have cream and eggs and pâté. And we love it! But we don't eat fast food, and, most important, we take time to eat. Even when we are in a hurry, we try to take forty-five minutes. We have our food, good company and our wine."

Would that wine include what is produced in New Mexico?

"There are $15, $20, and $25 wines in California that are not as good as some New Mexico wines for $9. But they have a name and that makes a difference. In France, it has taken three, four generations to build a name; in California, at least 25 years.

"New Mexico is new. It will take another couple of decades, I would say, because we started with a handicap—New Mexico. It will happen. We will get over that handicap. You will see."

WINES IN PRODUCTION

Under the Chateau Sassenage label:

Cabernet Sauvignon (the signature wine of the Chateau line); **Merlot; Chardonnay; Fumé Blanc** (made from Sauvignon Blanc grapes); and **White Zinfandel.**

Under the Sabine label:

Chardonnay (the signature wine of the Sabine label); **Cabernet Sauvignon; Pinot Noir; Riesling;** and **White Zinfandel.**

Under the Mont-Jallon label, two sparkling wines, *Méthode Champenoise:*

Brut (made from Chardonnay and Pinot Noir grapes, 90:10. Best of show, New Mexico State Fair,

1993); and **Blanc de Noirs** (100% Pinot Noir. Gold Medals at the Southwest Wine Competition, 1994, and the Taster's Guild International Wine Judging.)

Sabine Guillaume offers her recipe for *Poulet au Champagne* (Royal Chicken Breast) using Mont-Jallon sparkling wine, *Méthode Champenoise.*

Ingredients:

6 chicken breasts	2 Tb. olive oil
2 onions thinly sliced	6 med carrots sliced lengthwise
3 bay leaves	1/3 cup chopped fresh parsley
3 garlic cloves, sliced	1/2 tsp salt
1/2 tsp pepper	1/2 pint whipping cream

16 oz. fresh mushrooms, sautéed

1 bottle Mont-Jallon sparkling wine, *Méthode Champenoise.*

To Make the Marinade:

Brown chicken breasts in 2 tb. olive oil. Remove chicken and place it breast side down in a 9x13x1/2" dish and set aside. Sauté onions, carrots, parsley, garlic and bay leaves in the chicken drippings for 3 min. over a medium heat. Pour this mixture over the chicken. Add one bottle Mont-Jallon sparkling wine to the chicken and vegetables. Cover the dish and marinate in the refrigerator for 6 hours or overnight.

To Cook the Chicken:

Place the chicken, vegetables and all the liquid in a large skillet. Cook over medium heat uncovered for 1 hour. Remove the vegetables and spread them evenly over the bottom of a 2-3 quart serving dish. Place the chicken on top of the vegetables, breast-side up. Using 2 cups of the liquid from the skillet (add water, if necessary) add 1/2 pint whipping cream, salt, pepper, and mushrooms. Cook for 10 minutes on high heat, stirring occasionally. Pour 1/2 of the sauce mixture over the chicken. Pour the remainder into a separate serving dish to be added as desired.

Serve with Mont-Jallon sparkling wine, *Méthode Champenoise.*
Bon appetit!

Details: Chateau Sassenage. Founded 1983. Box 1606, Truth or Consequences, NM 87901. (505) 894-7244. Fax (505) 894-9156. Owners: European Investment Group. Manager/Wine maker: Jean-Marie Guillaume. The vineyard and winery are located at Engle, but wines may be tasted at the office in T or C. Advisable to call in advance.

THE TOUR CONTINUES

Regain the Interstate heading south toward Las Cruces, about seventy-five miles ahead. To make your return more pleasant, leave the Interstate at the first opportunity toward Arrey (State Road #187), and parallel the Interstate on this small country road that criss-crosses the Rio Grande as it passes through some of the most fertile land in the state. Cotton, lettuce, onions, alfalfa and red and green chile are grown here.

The small towns along this route—Arrey, Derry, Garfield and Salem—were all founded at the beginning of the century as small Rio Grande farming communities. Water from the Rio Grande was imported in irrigation ditches to the thirsty fields. As the Rio Grande rose with the spring melting of the snows in the southern Rockies, these communities were periodically flooded.

Arriving at Hatch, population 1,000, you are in the center of the Hatch and Rincon Valleys and at the heart of New Mexico's famous chile pepper industry.

The town of Hatch was named in 1880 after General Edward Hatch, commander of nearby old Ft. Thorne. The town was devastated by a flash flood in 1921, but bounced back with the help of the Elephant Butte and Caballo dams to become a major agricultural center.

Self-proclaimed as the 'Chile Pepper Capital of the World,' Hatch holds

Is It Chile Or Chili?

Depends on who you talk to, and where they're from.

Chile peppers were brought from South America by the Spanish and were grown in New Mexico long before they were in Texas or California.

As a rule, 'chile' refers to the plant and its fruit, while 'chili' is the stew made from the plant along with added ingredients.

Texans brag about their 'chili', a combination of beans and meat (armadillo or possum's the best, they claim) spiced with chile powder. New Mexicans tell you their 'chile's' the real thing.

Made of pure, whole green or red chile peppers, Hatch chiles are chopped or pureed, and served without artificial fillers (such as beans or meat).

Some say the red is hotter than the green, and some ask for Christmas, red and green side-by-side over their *burritos* or *huevos rancheros*. However you take it, you're not a green-or-red-blooded New Mexican until you've had your pure chile fix.

its annual Chile Festival on Labor Day weekend in celebration of the annual chile harvest. Hatch produces over a million pounds of No. 6-4 chile peppers, the state's top cash crop. It's shipped throughout the United States (mostly to Texas) and exported abroad.

Continuing south from Hatch, the road changes to #185, but not the scenery. You are paralleling both the Rio Grande and the Santa Fe Railroad as you head for Las Cruces, now thirty-seven miles south.

On the way to Doña Ana (Lady Ann), you will pass through Radium Springs, site of a women's prison. Doña Ana, at one time, was the seat of one of the original nine huge counties that stretched from Texas to Arizona and made up the New Mexico Territory of the 1850s. A few years later, the county seat was shifted to Las Cruces.

THE TOUR IS FINISHED

At Doña Ana, you are entering the outskirts of Las Cruces and the rich farm land of La Mesilla Valley. Continue south on #185 another five miles to the Old Mesilla Plaza and the end of our two-day tour of the southern wineries.

5

LAS FIESTAS DEL VINO DE NUEVO MEXICO

(The Wine Festivals of New Mexico)

Wine festivals and events around the state are listed by season.

SPRING

SANDIA SHADOWS SPRING WINE FESTIVAL

Over one weekend in mid-May, Sandia Shadows of Albuquerque holds its annual Spring Wine Festival, *La Fiesta Primavera del Vino*, featuring Mariachi music, local arts and crafts and foods paired with samplings of Sandia Shadows wines. Admission. For information: (505) 856-1006.

NEW MEXICO WINE AND CHILE WAR FESTIVAL

Held in Las Cruces over Memorial Day weekend, the Wine and Chile War Festival combines New Mexico wineries with a celebration of the chile war that exists between Texas and New Mexico. Commercial vendors, chefs and amateurs from both states armed with favorite recipes compete for the best chile dishes. A huge trophy is presented to the victorious state.

Entertainment, venders, crafts and artisans are also featured along with wines of New Mexico. For information, contact Bill Gomez at New Mexico State University, (505) 646-4543.

SOUTHWEST WINE CONFERENCE & CONNOISSEUR'S EVENING

For two days in mid-April, the New Mexico Vine and Wine Society sponsors a conference on Southwest wines at a major hotel in Albuquerque. Featured are lectures and workshops on topics pertaining to the wine industry in New Mexico and the Southwest.

In conjunction with the conference, on a Friday evening, is the Southwest Connoisseur's Evening pairing fine Southwest cuisine of the New Mexico Chef's Association with the wine of New Mexico wineries. Admission. For information and tickets: (505) 831-6135.

SUMMER

LAS GOLONDRINAS WINE FESTIVAL

Historic *El Rancho de Las Golondrinas* (the Ranch of the Swallows), located south of Santa Fé, in conjunction with the New Mexico Vine and Wine Society, hosts a 4th of July weekend to celebrate New Mexico history and wines.

Visitors may sample the products of all the state's wineries and stroll through the historic, restored buildings of the 17th century ranch, which, in the days of the Spanish, was the last overnight stop on the long, arduous 1,800 mile journey up *El Camino Real* before reaching Santa Fé. Admission. For information: (505) 831-6135, or 471-2261.

FALL

LA VIÑA WINE FESTIVAL

Held during the second weekend of October, La Viña wine festival is the oldest in the state, having been established in 1982. For two days, from noon until 8 pm, the grounds of the winery host Mariachis, folk ballet and local bands and entertainment along with vendors, artisans, local foods and selections of La Viña wines. Admission. Children 12 and under free. For information: (505) 882-7632.

NEW MEXICO WINE FESTIVAL AT BERNALILLO

Since 1987, Labor Day weekend (Saturday through Monday) finds New Mexico's wineries showcasing their products in the largest event of its kind in New Mexico. Along with area artisans, entertainers, agricultural products, a juried art show and Southwestern foods, the Bernalillo Festival provides an opportunity to sample the best of New Mexico wines. Admission. For information: (505) 867-3311.

SANTA FÉ CHILE & WINE FIESTA

Held during the annual chile harvest in September, the week-long Santa Fé Chile and Wine Fiesta pairs northern New Mexico foods with regional and national wines. Included are food and wine seminars, agricultural tours, guest chef cooking classes and the Big Event, an afternoon of tastings from Santa Fé's top restaurants paired with fine wines. Admission. For information and reservations: (505) 982-8686.

SANDIA SHADOWS JAZZ AND WINE FESTIVAL

Hot jazz and New Mexico wine pair up for one weekend in October coinciding with the Albuquerque International Balloon Fiesta. Sandia Shadows Winery sponsors the 'Jazz and Wine Festival,' featuring wine tastings and the music of local jazz groups along with crafts and food. Admission. For information: (505) 856-1006.

WINTER

TAOS WINTER WINE FESTIVAL

Since 1989, the Taos Ski Valley has served up a mountain of world-class ski slopes, excellent food and vintage wines from California, New Mexico and French cellars. This five-day event is usually held during the third week of January when the snows are deep, appetites rampant and wines mellow. Showcase dinners and seminars featuring national and international vintners are scheduled. Admission. For information and reservations: (505) 776-2291.

6

LAS CERVECERÍAS MUY PEQUEÑAS DE NUEVO MEXICO

(The Microbreweries of New Mexico)

Microbrewing is a budding industry in New Mexico. Since 1988, nine micros have popped up in Taos, Embudo Station, Santa Fé, Albuquerque and Las Cruces featuring such unique brews as Oat Coal Porter, Chicken Killer Barley Wine, Rio Grande Ristra and Old Avalanche.

The breweries are listed by city.

ALBUQUERQUE
Assets Grille & Brewing Company

Mark Matheson, brewmaster at Assets Grille, was originally trained in California as a wine maker, but had worked after hours at a brewpub in Sacramento. When the owners of Assets decided to install a microbrewery in the Spring of 1993, Mark signed on as the brewmaster after several years at wineries in both California and New Mexico.

Assets is a 1,500-barrel per year, ale-style brewpub, the first in Albuquerque. The pub also produces stouts and porters, as many as fifteen varieties during any given year. Matheson brews more for flavor than alcohol, stressing that his ales are a living product meant to be consumed on the premises and not transported.

He sees the resurgence of the brewpub in this country as bringing back many of the old world European styles, from the smoked porter and rye beers to the fruit-flavored ales that were lost during Prohibition. It's Mark's intention to be part of this resurgence.

Brews usually on tap include:

The Fruit That 'Ales' You—A fruit-flavored ale made with a variety of seasonal fruit flavors: cherry, orange-mango, raspberry, or cranberry.

Kaktus Külsch—A German-style ale originating in Cologne that has been fermented warm with top-fermenting ale yeast producing a medium bitterness and a slightly hoppy aroma.

Roadrunner Ale—Brewed in the tradition of great English bitter ales with a deep, golden color and a dry finish reminiscent of Fuggle hops.

Albuquerque Pale Ale—Matheson's tribute to the great ale from Burton, England. Fuggle and Goldings hops give this brew a distinctive tang.

Duke City Amber—Assets' best selling brew is a satisfying, darker ale with a roasted malt character.

Pablo's Porter—A smooth and rich brew made from Chinook and Galena hops with a slightly bitter taste.

Ol' Avalanche Barley Wine—An ale brewed with double the hops, even though it is characterized by a malty sweetness. A great fireside beer after a winter's day.

* * * * * * *

Details: Assets Grille and Brewing Co. Owners: Russ Ziegler, Doug Smith and Don Goodenough. Brewmaster: Mark Matheson. Founded 1993. Open from 11:30 am through dinner, daily. Located at 6910 Montgomery Blvd. NE, Albuquerque, NM. 87109. (505) 889-6400.

Rio Bravo Restaurant & Brewery

Brad Kraus, brewmaster for Rio Bravo and one of the few master beer judges in the country, slipped into brewing as a hobby, eventually winning several national awards.

A native of New Mexico, Brad attended Rice University in Houston and stayed on to work in the city. A friend at the time was a home brewer. When she told him she couldn't make enough for the two of them, Brad jumped into the hobby.

He returned to New Mexico in 1990 to brew for the Santa Fe Brewing Company, and formulated many of the brews they now offer. Three years later, Rio Bravo hired Brad to set up and run the brewing operation for their downtown brewpub.

The secret to great brewing, according to Brad, is attention to detail. When the little things start to slide the problems compound and it shows in the product. Brad believes in exploring new recipes but realizes to hold on to loyal customers, he must offer a core of at least three standards: Coronado Gold (a golden ale), High Desert Pale Ale, and the Esteban Dark (a porter).

Brews on tap:

Coronado Gold—A light, refreshing golden ale with a toasty flavor of Munich malt and a clean, dry hop finish.

High Desert Pale Ale—A copper colored, spicy ale with a slight bitterness from Chinook and Cascade hops balanced with a floral hop aroma.

Esteban Dark—A lusty, malty, dark ale in the Porter style with a mellow roastiness and hints of licorice and chocolate.

Old Town Ale—An old English-style ale with a rounder, fuller body and a mellower taste with a caramel malt flavor.

McMinn Ninety Schilling Ale—A heavier Scottish ale, bronze in color and very malty.

King's Russian Imperial Stout—A rich, robust, but sweeter style porter originally made for the Russian Imperial Court, but named in honor of Martin Luther King.

*   *   *   *   *   *   *

Details: Rio Bravo Restaurant and Brewery. Owners: Frank and Lisa Smith, and Dave Richards. Brewmaster: Brad Kraus. Located at 515 Central Ave. NW. Hours: Mon-Sat, 11:30 am-11:00 pm, Sun 11-2 am. Albuquerque, NM 87102. (505) 242-6800

Rio Grande Microbrewery

When Tom Hart decided being a Presbyterian minister was not the career he had imagined, he joined forces with Scott Moore in 1993 to establish Rio Grande Brewing Company, the newest micro in Albuquerque. Moore took the lead in managing the business while Hart was annointed 'Brewpastor.' When a third partner, Matt Shappell, came on board, the management team was complete.

Rio Grande was born out of a 'hobby-gone-mad,' as Hart tells it. With ten years of home brewing under their belts (Tom is a certified national beer judge), and with the national trend moving toward hand-crafted beer, it was time to test the commercial market. The trio rigged a twenty-eight barrel system on the site of an abandoned winery and set an initial production goal of 1,500 barrels for their first year (1994), and 3,000 barrels for the second.

The philosophy of Rio Grande is to brew a refreshing summer lager for the warm southwestern climate but with enough robustness to withstand the winter. The brewery packages 12 oz. bottles and half-kegs for off-site consumption. Production to date consists of a single brew, but pilsners and bocks are in the works.

> **Outlaw Lager**—An amber lager brewed from five different grains and three different hops in the steam beer tradition. It is an assertively hopped brew, with good malt character and mid-strength in alcohol.

*   *   *   *   *   *   *

Details: Rio Grande Brewing Co. Owners, Scott Moore, Thomas Hart & Matthew Shappell. Brewpastor: Thomas Hart. Founded 1993. Hours, daily except weekends, 8-5. Located at 3760 Hawkins NE, Albuquerque, NM 87109. (505) 343-0903. (Carry out only)

EMBUDO STATION
Embudo Station Brewery

In 1983, when Preston Cox stumbled onto the remains of the abandoned Embudo railroad station along the banks of the Rio Grande, it was love at first sight. From the 1880s until before WW II, a narrow gauge railway, known as the 'Chile Line,' had operated from southern Colorado into Santa Fé hauling passengers as well as bags of green chiles from farm to market.

Preston, with his wife Sandy, moved into what was left of the build-ings and soon established a restaurant under the cottonwoods on the banks of the river, along with a smokehouse, gift shop and art gallery. As there were no beer and wine restaurant licenses to be had in the county, the only way to sell it was to make it. And so they did in 1988. The old depot became the brewery.

The brewery produces nearly 100 barrels a year and features about twenty different brews during any given season, although the following are usually on tap:

> **Narrow Gauge Ale**—A 'steam style' beer reminiscent of San Francisco's Anchor Steam beer. It has a sparkling amber brown color with a highly hopped taste that leaves a clean, pine-like after taste. A thirst quencher on a hot summer day.
> **Embudo Gold**—A light ale made with domestic and imported malts and hops, which produce a clear, golden color and a bread-like taste and finish similar to many fine imported beers.

Copper Ale—An English-style ale that is lighter and rosier in color with fewer hops than traditional ales. A smooth-drinking brew with a distinctive copper color.

Rio Grande Green—A light, golden ale to which locally grown and roasted green chiles are added in the fermenting process to produce the signature brew of Embudo Station. It is a drink that is both cool and hot at the same time and continues to attract loyal customers.

Rio Grande Red—A smooth, amber ale spiced with the distinctive flavors of red chile ristra pods producing a brew that is a little smoother, darker and milder than its cousin, Rio Grande Green.

Railroaders Stout—A deep, dark chocolatey, medium-dry brew made with roasted barleys, dark malts and three varieties of hops: Cascade, Mount Hood and Northern Brewer producing a complex, rich flavor.

* * * * * * *

Details: Embudo Station Brewery. Owner: Preston Cox. Brewmaster: Brandon Santos. Founded 1988. Located at Embudo Station, NM on Highway #68, forty-one miles north of Santa Fé and 25 miles south of Taos. Open April-November, 12-8 pm. Box 154, Embudo, NM 87531. (505) 852-4707.

LAS CRUCES

O'Ryans Tavern & Bewerey

After several years as an amateur brewer, Dave Million enrolled in the brewing program at the University of California, Davis, where he trained for several weeks before touring Mexico to study Mexican-style brewing. Returning home, Dave became head brewer of Las Cruces' first brewpub in the spring of 1994.

Why the Mexican influence? Because Las Cruces is less than an hour's drive from the border and Mexican beer is popular with his clientele. Owner John Ritter thought it worth integrating the secrets of Mexican-style brewing, which emphasizes a dryer, all malt brew with more hops, into the American-style ales produced at O'Ryans.

The brewery has a seven-barrel system producing 56 barrels per month. While all beer is on draft, the brewery also sells half-gallon jugs, five-gallon kegs and 15.5-gallon kegs to go. The following ales and stouts are brewed at O'Ryan's:

> **Dog Spit Stout**—An imperial stout fashioned after the English stout brewed for the Russian Imperial Court in the 18th century. It's a dark, heavy brew with 8-10% alcohol. O'Ryan's flagship beer.
>
> **Red Dog Pale Ale**—Brewed with Chico ale yeast producing a fruity, clean taste.
>
> **Springfest**—A brown ale with a high malt content that tastes like a bock.
>
> **Organ Mountain Weizen**—A Dunkleweizen served with lemon.
>
> **Organ Mountain Gold**—A light, golden ale with more body and hops than commercial beers, but made to compete with the commercial product.
>
> Seasonal beers are also available.

*　*　*　*　*　*　*

Details: O'Ryans Tavern & Brewery. Owners: C.W. Ritter and son, John. Head brewer: Dave Million. Brewer: Jason Mihalic. Brewery founded 1994. Located in Mesilla Valley Mall between J C Penny and Walgreens drugstore. 700 S. Telshor Blvd. Las Cruces, NM 88001. Open daily. (505) 522-8191. Serving American, Southwestern, Irish-American and Health Foods.

Old West Brewery

As if Hervé Lescombes weren't busy enough as the wine maker for Blue Teal, St. Clair and Mademoiselle de Santa Fe wineries, he has thrown himself into the microbrewery business.

Gathering excess equipment from his many operations and borrowing from his skills as a vintner, Hervé, with the help of his sons, Emmanuel and Florent, has converted the old Sun Winery building into one of the newest brewpubs in New Mexico.

Just minutes north of Old Mesilla Plaza on Highway 28, the building is large enough to accommodate both a microbrewery and a restaurant combining Western and French motifs. During warm nights, extra seating is available outside next to a garden of grapevines left over from the winery. The brewery operates with a 10-barrel system and offers brews on tap, in kegs and bottles.

Old West features five brews: **Santa Fe Ale, Pale Ale, Mesilla Golden Ale, Maibock, Western Wheat**, and a **Porter**.

* * * * * * *

Details: Owners: Hervé and Danielle Lescombes. Brewmaster: Hervé Lescombes and sons. Founded 1994. Located on Highway #28 about one mile north of Old Mesilla Plaza. Open daily noon-10 pm. (Scheduled to open Fall of 1994.)

SANTA FE

Russell Brewing Company

Rob Russell has been home brewing and dreaming of running his own microbrewery since 1960. A few years ago, when a friend gave him an airline ticket to anywhere Southwest Airlines flew, Rob ended up in Albuquerque. He migrated up the hill to Santa Fé to investigate the possibility of establishing a microbrewery. A couple of years later he moved to Santa Fé, collected equipment, and produced his first batch of ale in August of 1992.

Russell imports his hops from the Northwest, the grain from Wisconsin, the yeast from Oregon and the bottles from Mexico.

Currently, Russell Brewing distributes about 300 cases a month to Taos, Santa Fé and Albuquerque with an eventual goal of 600 cases per month.

The brewery currently features two stock brews:

Black Cloud Porter—An American porter made from eight or nine different grains. The roasted barley taste comes through along with some chocolate. It's lighter than many porters produced by other micros.

La Cañada Pale Ale—An American pale ale, lighter in body than the traditional English varieties. It's an all-grain, bottle conditioned and unfiltered brew. It has more of a malty taste but with a hop balance.

* * * * * * *

Details: Russell Brewing Co. Owner/Brewmaster: Rob Russell. Assistant: Chrissy McCausland. Founded 1983. Located at 1242 Siler Road, Warehouse #2, Santa Fé, NM 87501. Operating daily except weekends, 9-5 p.m. (505) 438-3138.

Santa Fe Brewing Company

In addition to having one of the few female brewmasters in the United States at its helm, the Santa Fe Brewing Co. is also the oldest micro in the state. Founded in 1988 in a horsebarn on an old quarter horse ranch with equipment purchased from the Boulder Brewery, Laure Pomianowski produces all-malt ales that are hand-brewed, hand-bottled and hand-labeled.

With production at the 1,000 barrels-a-year level, the brewery ships its signature Santa Fe Pale Ale throughout the state, into Colorado and as far east as Washington D.C., where it is featured in Mark Miller's restaurant, Red Sage. Other brews available on the premises are:

Fiesta Ale—A copper colored ale modeled after the 19th century British ale shipped to colonial India. The higher hop and alcohol content enabled it to make the long sea voyage.

Santa Fe Nut Brown Ale—A light chocolate malt taste and aroma.

Old Pojoaque Porter—More full-bodied than the pale ale with a distinct chocolate flavor without being sweet.

Galisteo Weiss—A very light, straw-colored, wheat beer made from malted wheat and barley. Perfect for a summer brew.

Chicken Killer Barley Wine—A deep, copper-colored English-style, strong barley ale with 8-10% alcohol.

Sangre de Frambuesa—A distinctly ruby-colored ale made by combining three pounds of raspberries per gallon of beer.

Hogback Stout—A British imperial stout with a sweet as opposed to an Irish-dry finish, made in the style of the 19th century British beer exported to Tzarist Russia. It is heavier in alcohol and hops to withstand travel.

*   *   *   *   *   *   *

Details: Santa Fe Brewing Co. Owner: Michael Levis. Brewmaster: Laure Pomianowski. Founded 1988. Located about 20 miles south of Santa Fé on the Flying M Ranch at the north edge of the village of Galisteo (take U.S. Highway #285 south, then right on county road #41, first left after mile marker 58). Open weekdays 9-5 p.m., and during the summer, on Saturdays, 10-4 p.m. HC 75, Box 83, Galisteo, NM 87540 (505) 988-2340.

TAOS

Eske's BrewPub

Steve Eskeback (nicknamed Eske) moved from Washington state in 1981, at the beginning of the microbrewing revolution, and couldn't find beers in New Mexico that suited his taste. So he began brewing his own in the kitchen of a Taos restaurant.

A few years later, while still an amateur, Steve took a swing back through the Northwest visiting eleven micros and brewpubs to refine his technique. He found his brews compared favorably with some of the best in the West. Returning to Taos, Steve assembled the equipment for a brewery along with a business plan and went looking for a place to lease.

With the idea of a hometown pub where friends and strangers alike could congregate and spend a relaxing evening, Steve Eske opened his doors in 1992 with an initial production of 42 barrels. Two years later production had jumped to 433 barrels.

Steve brews over twenty-five different stouts and ales throughout the year with about six available at any one time. Among his most popular brews are:

Dead President's Cherry Delight—A special red brew made for President's day in honor of Washington and Lincoln. Contains cherries and raspberries.

Taos Green Chili—Brewed with fresh roasted New Mexico green chiles, this brew has a wonderfully aromatic taste and just a little zing of an afterbite. Best of Show, 1990 New Mexico State Fair. Bronze Medal, 1993 Great American Beer Festival (fruit & vegetable category).

10,000 Foot Stout—Originally brewed at 10,000 foot altitude, this brew is a Russian imperial-style stout—black, rich, thick and made from a blend of caramel malts, chocolate and roasted barley.

Artist Ale—An ordinary style English bitter, the national drink of England. It is more flavorful and hoppy than an American-style pilsner.

Taos Mountain Gold—Eske's version of a Vienna-style lager made with Munich malt and Mt. Hood spicy hops. It is more a German-style beer.

Mesa Pale Ale—An India-style ale, highly hopped with a high specific gravity. It's a big, assertive beer.

Oat Cole Porter—A dark-style, easy drinking beer with oats for sweetness and chocolatey malts.

* * * * * *

Details: Eske's Brewpub. Owner/Brewmaster: Steve Eskeback. Founded 1992. Open daily, noon-10 pm. Located off the main plaza in the historic district of Taos at 106 De Georges Lane, Taos, NM 87571 (505) 758-1517.

INDEX

Travel/Wine Notes

Travel/Wine Notes

ORDERING INFORMATION

To order additional copies of EXPLORING NEW MEXICO WINE COUN-TRY, send a check or money order for $12.95 plus $2.50 for shipping/handling ($15.45 total) (.75 shipping/handling for each additional book) to:

Coyote Press
Box 267-1
Los Cerrillos, New Mexico   87010

For qualified wholesale orders contact

GANNON   DISTRIBUTING   COMPANY
PHONE 1-800-442-2044
FAX 1-800-851-1543

                      *   *   *
*   *   *   *   *
    *   *

TO ORDER

THE LION IN THE MOON: *TWO AGAINST THE SAHARA*
          Rainbow Books, Inc.   ISBN   1-56825-006-1

CALL   1-800-356-9315